'The essen... ... *Times*

'Corinne Maier's del... ...rporate life' ...*pendent*

'This revolutionary title . . . this witty slackers' guide will tell you all you need to know about how to do zero – and get away with it!' *OK*

'Deeply cynical but perceptive and amusing . . . a refreshing antidote to the rash of American motivational books pushing you to work harder . . . full of literary references as well as nuggets of wisdom from contemporary philosophers. In fact, it would make you want to read great French thinkers all day . . . Read this book and laugh – preferably on company time! Just don't let the boss see you being so subversive'

Irish Examiner, Book of the Week

'She writes wittily about pointless meetings, the meaningless language and arbitrary rules . . . Her slim volume is an anti-help manual. Its brief chapters can easily be digested during any brainstorming sessions people can't find an excuse to get out of . . . pithily written'

Phil Chamberlain, *Tribune*

'In this short, ferocious and richly entertaining book . . . Maier generates belly laughs of recognition with her aperçus into the corporate world . . . bracingly great stuff . . . an excellent and salutary read' *European Business*

Corinne Maier used to work as an economist. Not long after the publication of *Bonjour Laziness* in France, she was sacked by her then employer, a major French utilities company. Her time is now dedicated to writing and to psychoanalysis. *Bonjour Laziness* is a bestseller in France, where it has sold almost 300,000 copies. It is also a bestseller in Spain, Germany and Italy, and has been sold in 30 countries and languages. Corinne Maier has published ten books altogether, five of which have been or will be translated into other languages. Her latest book, *Intello Academy*, is a tongue-in-cheek look at French intellectuals, and is every bit as controversial as *Bonjour Laziness*.

BONJOUR LAZINESS

WHY HARD WORK DOESN'T PAY

CORINNE MAIER

TRANSLATED BY GREG MOSSE

2013 → TAURO

An Orion paperback

First published in France in 2004
by Editions Michalon
under the title *Bonjour Paresse*
First published in Great Britain in 2005
by Orion
This paperback edition published in 2006
by Orion Books Ltd,
Orion House, 5 Upper St Martin's Lane,
London WC2H 9EA

1 3 5 7 9 10 8 6 4 2

The author and publisher wish to thank www.CartoonStock.com
for their kind permission to reproduce their cartoons.

Every effort has been made to fulfil requirements with regard to
reproducing copyright material. The author and publisher will be glad
to rectify any omissions at the earliest opportunity.

A CIP catalogue record for this book is available
from the British Library.

ISBN-13 978-0-7528-7764-8
ISBN-10 0-7528-7764-X

Printed and bound in Great Britain by
Mackays of Chatham plc, Chatham, Kent

The Orion Publishing Group's policy is to use papers that
are natural, renewable and recyclable products and
made from wood grown in sustainable forests. The logging
and manufacturing processes are expected to conform to
the environmental regulations of the country of origin.

www.orionbooks.co.uk

CONTENTS

BONJOUR LAZINESS

INTRODUCTION

BUSINESS HAS NO SYMPATHY FOR THE INDIVIDUAL

'It's quite obvious that
you're not a team player.'

'NEVER WORK,' SAID GUY DEBORD, the situationist philosopher. Good idea, but easier said than done. Most mornings, most people meekly toddle off to work in business and, since this is where most of the jobs are, the majority of them work for Big Business. But, oddly, the corporate world is a mysterious one, taboo even. So, let's call a spade a spade for once and tell it how it is.

Hear ye, hear ye, middle managers in big companies! This book is designed to demoralise you, to lower your spirits. It will help you to take advantage of the business that employs you, whereas, up to now, that business has taken advantage of you. It will show you that it is in your interest to work as little as possible. It will teach you to undermine the system from within – without seeming to.

Is *Bonjour Laziness* cynical? Oh yes, certainly. But then, business has no sympathy for the individual. It doesn't have your interests at heart and consistently fails to practise what it preaches. Look at the financial scandals fighting for column inches on the business pages. Look at the reams of unread paperwork documenting workers' rights.

Business is no fun, except, as is the case here, when we decide to have fun at its expense.

CAN YOU DISSOLVE BUSINESS IN THE ACID OF DISENCHANTMENT?

Millions of people work in business but its universe is opaque. This is because those who talk about it most – university professors[1] – have never actually worked there. They don't know. And those who do know bite their tongues. The consultants who couldn't wait to leave and start their own companies keep schtum for fear of sawing through the branch they are sitting on. The same goes for management gurus – generous with business advice, prompting ludicrous fads they don't themselves believe in. And this is the reason writing on business management is so indigestible – like textbooks on constitutional law in politics.

Nevertheless there are a few voices trying hard to tell business like it is. Novels came first, setting their plots on the deep-pile carpets of Arthur Andersen's luxurious corridors (filed for bankruptcy 2002) or in the (apparently impregnable) Gan Tower in the La Défense Paris business district. And I say well done – because it isn't easy to imagine Romeo and Juliet talking cash flow and management, closing a deal, setting up a joint venture, evaluating synergies and drawing flow charts. Business, it is true, is not the natural home of noble passions such as courage, generosity or devotion to the common good. Business doesn't open new mental horizons. Although I wonder, I wonder . . . If it isn't the best place for hard workers to come together and really get things done, why is it that the best qualified people from higher education flex their talented muscles in business – especially big business?

When I started work, business was all the rage. It seemed capable of embodying both aspirational values and the student protests of May 1968. Alas, I soon learned the contrary. I have now been in business for quite some time and have come to the conclusion that they lied to us. There is no va-va-voom in business. It isn't just boring – it is sometimes brutal. We saw its true colours when the dot.com bubble burst and in the financial scandals that newspapers salivate over. The collapse in stock prices at Vivendi, France Télécom, Alcatel and others rubbed salt in the wounds, diminishing the capital of millions of workers who, until then, had rejoiced with slack-jawed trust in the gung-ho speeches of their managers. Worst of all were the massacres of 2003 – business's true dark side: mass redundancies at STMicroelectronics, Alcatel, Matra, Schneider Electric . . .

Business is so over. The evidence is incontrovertible: it is no longer where we look for success stories. Society's lift is out of order. Qualifications no longer guarantee employment. Pensions are threatened. Careers are no longer predictable. The 1960s – energised by technological advances and jobs for life – are a fading memory. The wind has changed and hordes of overqualified workers are already scratching around for modest – but secure – jobs in the public sector.

Business no longer portrays itself as the future. The generations that follow ours will need more and more qualifications to qualify for less and less fulfilling jobs, to undertake less and less motivating tasks. I've already explained this to my son and daughter: 'My darlings, when you are big, don't go to work in business. Just don't. Daddy and Mummy would be so disappointed!'

Given the absence of any future as an individual or in society, the children of the middle classes – who make up the recruiting ground for managers – could well slope off right now. How? By choosing career paths less fully integrated into the capitalist system (in the arts, science or education . . .) or by taking a step back from commerce, flicking it a casual finger as they go. That's what I did. I only work part time now and spend the better part of my days on much more stimulating occupations.[2] Follow my lead, junior executives, salaried colleagues, semi-slaves of the tertiary sector, ancilliaries in economic life. Join me, my brothers and sisters, led by the nose by your dull, obsequious bosses, obliged to dress up like clowns all week and fritter away your time in pointless meetings and worthless seminars.

In the meantime – and because your escape needs a little forward planning – why not corrupt the system from within? Half-heartedly imitate middle-management behaviour. Ape their vocabulary and their mannerisms without 'committing' yourself. You won't be the first.

According to a recent IFOP survey,[3] 17 per cent of French executives are 'actively disengaged' from their work, which means that their attitude is so un-constructive as to approach sabotage . . . Only 3 per cent of French managers axiomatically declare that they 'give everything' at work and think of themselves as 'actively engaged'. That's not many, as I'm sure you'll agree. As for the others, members of neither of these groups, the business must go all out to motivate them − witness the burgeoning number of seminars designed to reinvigorate these worn out managers.

When you start asking yourself how you can persuade your staff to roll their sleeves up, it's clear that they no longer give a damn. My grandfather was in trade − a self-made man. He never got up in the morning and asked himself if he was 'motivated'. He went to work, that's all.

Adopting a policy of 'active disengagement' will not bring you grief, as long as you are discreet. In any case, the spineless incompetents who surround you are unlikely to notice your lack of dedication. You can be sure that if, by chance, someone does notice something, they won't dare speak out. Because having to punish you would give your manager two problems: firstly it would make public the fact that he or she hasn't been managing you; and secondly, any blot on your record will make it harder for you to find another post! Some glittering promotions have resulted from this tradition of corporate *omertà*. Your betters will do anything to hide the problem, including kicking you upstairs. One small step for man, one giant leap for hypocrisy . . .

Pierre de Coubertin said that the important thing was taking part. Today the important thing is to take part as little as possible. Who knows, perhaps that will be enough to bring the system to its knees. Communists sat twiddling their thumbs for 70 years and eventually the Berlin Wall collapsed . . . Moreover, let's face facts: revolution will change nothing because humanity can't stop repeating the same mistakes – unnecessary paperwork, bosses of unsurpassed mediocrity and, in times of genuine crisis when people get really excited, the gallows. These are the three udders of history (does history have udders?)

Here are a few principles to help you understand the business world as it really is – and not as it pretends to be.

A NEW UNDERSTANDING FROM
A NEW STANDPOINT

In business, when someone says something to you or gives you something to read, there are a certain number of keys you must apply to pierce its meaning. Learning these codes will give you a fresh standpoint from which to understand all aspects of the business world – because, in business, spoken and written communication uses its own special language. And it uses it badly. But, so what? That just makes the job of decoding and understanding it that much more amusing.

Reverse the signs. The more a major business talks about something, the less there is of it. For example, skills are 'safeguarded' just before they finally disappear. 'Autonomy' is the buzzword when trifling orders require forms in triplicate and you must canvas six separate opinions before taking some insignificant decision. 'Ethics' are central to a company that believes in absolutely nothing.

The circular argument. In business, arguments are circular, like a serpent eating its own tail. Take any idea and follow it to its conclusion, and without fail you end up back where you started. Business is a world in which, very often, the outcome of work is a meeting and action is the final goal of action (unless it's the other way round).

Distinguish stupidity from lies. In business, making judgements of this kind is fantastically hard. Experience will teach you that sometimes the answer is . . . why not both? For example, when your bosses tell you 'people are our greatest resource' or 'your ideas are important to us', that's just blather. Everyone knows that such a world doesn't exist. On the other hand, what sort of idiot would be taken in by: 'With us you will find fulfilment in a variety of skills and ventures, taking responsibility for a range of innovative projects'? And when a manager says 'I've heard nothing about that' or 'I operate an open-door policy' – that's generally a tissue of lies too. The alliance of stupidity and hypocrisy is a powerful tool of modern management – it has been pompously christened 'neo-management'.

Be realistic. If, in normal circumstances, an objective is realistic, in business it becomes difficult. If, in everyday life, it is merely difficult, at work it becomes utterly impossible. For example, it is possible to predict the certain failure of any large-scale reorganisation and of any project taking more than two years, as well as, finally, any action that has never previously been undertaken.

Keep a sense of perspective. Things and events must be understood in context. A business cannot be separated from the world in which it prospers – or, as things stand, declines. The corporate milieu is simply symptomatic of a world drowning in lies, endlessly delaying its *coup de grâce* with vast bribes and a nonsense language bolstered by wild gesticulation.

WARNING:
GENUINE INDIVIDUALS NEED NOT APPLY

My fellow individualist, my brother in arms and in my heart, this book is not for you because business is not for you. Working in a large corporation serves only to enchain the individual who, left to his or her own devices, following their own whims, might begin to reflect and to doubt. Even – who knows? – to contest the established order. And that cannot be allowed. In business, although the individual may sometimes bring the benefit of new ideas, they must never be allowed to destabilise the group. In a world where – supposedly – flexibility is the watchword, in truth it is the ability to present and shoulder arms in time with all the others that is admired.

True individuals bring trouble, foment discord. Business prefers cowards, negligible yes-men who keep their heads down, play the game and sing the company song. People who, finally, dig themselves in without drawing attention to themselves.

Distrust of the feral individualist is justified. Not only are they incapable of blindly following others' lead but, having settled judgements of their own, they scorn compromise. HRD (human resource departments) see them coming a mile off. The graphologist's report calls them inflexible, obstinate and stubborn. And that – refusing to bend with the wind – is a 'bad thing'. It's also bad to leave the office the moment the day's work is done. Bad not to go for a drink at Christmas or bring cakes in on Twelfth Night. Bad not to put something in Mrs Overall's retirement envelope. Bad to go straight back to the hotel after the meeting with our Taiwanese partners. Bad not to drink your coffee in the designated coffee break. Bad to bring a packed lunch when everyone else eats in the canteen.

Colleagues consider people who behave like this as no better than the office cactus. Friendliness – joining in – is mandatory, as are shared jokes, shared drinks and hypocritical, air-kissing familiarity. (Learn to pretend or find yourself excluded.) On the other hand, perhaps the cacti are right. Perhaps they have properly grasped the dividing line that should exist between work and private life. Perhaps they have understood that being constantly available for a succession of unlikely projects – half of them utterly barmy and half of them utterly moronic – is a little like changing sexual partner twice a year. At twenty you are reasonably keen but, as the years roll by, to be honest it becomes a chore.

And that, in a word, is neo-management – compulsory erections.

Here, in six chapters, are all the reasons you'll ever need to disengage.

I

BUSINESS SPEAKS A REPELLENT NO-MAN'S LANGUAGE

© CartoonStock

'I'll start with the weekly progress report.
Ms London, on my right, will act as
acronym and jargon translator.'

THE THING YOU NOTICE first in business is what we call in French the *langue de bois* - the wooden tongue - a deadly, jargon-filled business-ese. I admit that business doesn't have the monopoly on this. We live in a jargon-filled world where psychoanalysts, academics and the media excel. But business-ese is the most oppressive of all. It can even discourage the Stakhanovite hero-worker that sleeps within you. (If you don't know what Stakhanovite means, read on with a light heart. Stakhanov doesn't figure in this book's cast list and you won't see many in business. They used to have Stakhanovites in the Soviet Union, but no one knows what became of them.)

JIBBERISH – EXCELLENT!

When I started work, I didn't understand anything my colleagues said to me. It took me a while to realise that was quite normal. Michel Houellebecq quotes a wonderful example of their ludicrous patois, emblematic of an entire generation (mine!): 'Before getting settled in this office, someone gave me a voluminous report entitled "Outline scheme of the ICT plan for the Ministry of Agriculture." . . . It focused, according to the introduction, on an "attempt to predefine different archetypal scenarios, conceived with a target-objective approach". ... I quickly leafed through the work, underlining the funniest sentences in pencil. For example: "The strategic level consists of the construction of an overarching information system built through the integration of distributed heterogeneous sub-systems".'[4]

That's it – the wooden tongue. Language reduced to absolute zero, where words no longer mean anything at all.

The corporate world has a dream: human language, far from being a window or a mirror, as certain overexcited intellectuals would have it, is simply a 'tool'. Once you grasp the key, it becomes just coded information. This fantasy of transparent, rational speech that can be grasped without equivocation or ambiguity has led to the no-man's language.

Because it's supposed to be free of passion, prejudice or imagination, no-man's language clothes itself in an aura of scientific impartiality. Words no longer signify. They conceal the links between events and obscure their causes. No-man's language is deliberately opaque and un-intelligible, the consumptive cousin of pseudo-scientific twaddle.

Of course, this is ideal for an audience that only feels truly well-informed when lost in an intellectual fog. The more abstract and technical business language becomes, the more the public seems to believe in it. I call it *priguistics* – a word of my own invention made up of *priggish* and *linguistics* – and business uses and abuses it.

The corporate wooden tongue is a rigid parallel commentary on the real world. Yes, the cogs are turning, but stiffly, predictably, giving the impression that there are no human beings involved: 'A supervisory unit has been put in place'; 'An information programme has been drawn up'; 'A balance sheet has been established'. You get the distinct impression that, in business, nothing actually happens.

The impersonal mode of expression, with its emphasis on the process, makes us feel safe. Nothing can occur. Peace in our time? In the middle manager's office, at least. No alarms and no surprises – except, perhaps, the P45. History with a capital H is for other people, the underclasses living on the margins of civilised society who can be relied on to start killing one another when they've nothing better to occupy their days.

Only the highly talkative Communist system has proved more adept than business in the wooden tongue. George Orwell, the visionary author of *1984,* was the first to understand that Soviet jargon wasn't laughable and inoffensive like all the others, but rather an ideological attempt to change language altogether. He spotted the role played by *newspeak* in the function of the totalitarian state. And business too is totalitarian – although in a spineless way. Business doesn't pretend that work will set you free – '*Arbeit macht frei*' in the sinister German phrase inscribed over the gates of Auschwitz – but you will come across a few hypocrites who dare to say it does.

The real problem is how leaden business jargon denies and obscures individual style: every memo and every note must conceal – not reveal – its author's identity. Each and every company demands an oh-so-polite text style which pays due respect to the ritual (wooden) tongue. The common house style takes over. Whatever the subject, the substance is steamrollered by the form. There's no ownership. Words simply repeat other words previously spoken. It isn't surprising you nod off. It is the sole known example of language being surgically separated from thought and yet – at least for the time being – refusing to die of its wounds.

The language of business follows five basic rules:

Complexity not simplicity. 'Initialise' is used instead of 'start', which sounds much too trivial. 'Finalise' replaces the ordinary 'finish' and 'position' substitutes for the down to earth 'place'.

The choice of words inflates true importance. 'Co-ordinate' and 'optimise' have more impact than 'implement'. But, winning by a short head from 'control' and 'head up', 'decide' is king of the verbs. And there is no shortage of words ending in '-nce': consequence, competence, experience, coherence, excellence – all words giving an appearance of importance.

Grammar is an old-fashioned irrelevance. Business abuses

language with an excess of circumlocutions, bloats its sentence structure, and drapes itself in a vast armoury of technical and administrative terms. The French language in particular is radically undermined because business loves to corrupt existing words. For example, *décliner* – to decline – isn't used in its established sense. *'Décliner'* a logo, a message or a concept doesn't mean that you bring them down in value; it means that the people below you in the hierarchy adopt them. In the same way, managers constantly use the Anglicism *solutionner* in place of the genuine French verb *résoudre* – to solve – because it puts on a better show.

It is the expression of the politics of a faceless authority. There is no attempt to convince, to prove or to seduce. Uncontested truths are handed down without any value judgements. To what end? To make you obey. Remember, it was Hitler's right-hand man Goebbels who said: 'We do not speak in order to say something, but to obtain a certain effect.' Indeed, business newspeak is often halfway between so-called scientific objectivity and the abrupt certainties of the political slogan. Here's how it goes: 'Co-operation between centres *must* improve'; 'It is *essential* that our new operational models are implemented before the deadline'; 'Following through on the objectives defined by our service mission *will continue to be* a priority'.

It takes only well-worn paths, their tiniest details mapped in advance. Even if, of itself, business language means nothing, it can still be decoded: a text or a communiqué only gives up its true sense in its departures from an implicit code. Each derogation from the ritual reveals something. If you have nothing better to do at work, you could at least become an expert in the wooden tongue . . .

Business language governs us and tries to think on our behalf. It recasts employees as mere devices: Hey, robot, get up and work! Give us your ideas, your feelings and your ambitions only in tables and graphs. Your labour is merely a 'process' to be rationalised.

But there is a price to pay for undermining language. When words seem unreliable, when it is hard to sort truth from lies and stem the rumour mill, suspicion reigns. Many workers entertain the paranoid delusion that they are the victims of a vast conspiracy organised by their bosses. What monster lurks beneath the fact that their bosses speak the same wooden tongue as *Pravda*, the organ of official Soviet truth? Sometimes they are right but, often, the reality is much simpler. Their bosses talk like that because they have been trained to do so. Some have even been selected especially for their fluency in business pidgin. And everyone behaves as if this is quite natural.

Many of our superiors could do with a course in 'French as mother tongue'. Unfortunately it isn't on the company's list of approved training schemes. But you will find neuro-linguistic programming (NLP) and other worthless methods designed to keep us talking and think-ing in circles.

ACRONYMS: A WASTELAND, A JUNGLE –
WHAT AM I SAYING? – A LABYRINTH

Business newspeak is more off-putting than most because everybody talks in acronyms. The wooden tongue has made some words disappear but has also created a mass of abbreviated, truncated neologisms, regardless of how dreadful they sound. The names of units, teams and services are acronyms. This is the sort of thing you hear in meetings: 'The AGIR is now IPN, which in turn heads up the STI, despite the SSII objections because it no longer controls the DM, and which will soon be on RTI in any case.' Just one hour of this sort of canteen conversation is enough to drive you barmy. But it has a purpose: to make those who understand the acronyms believe they belong to a privileged minority – initiates on the inside track.

It's a complete waste of time trying to learn these coded acronyms. They change all the time – with every company reorganisation whose goal is to shuffle all the cards then deal everyone exactly – but precisely! – the same hand. What this burgeoning harvest of ab-breviations really shows is that the restructuring, the mergers and the acquisitions have made businesses so nightmarishly labyrinthine and complex that the needle has lost its haystack. Internal competition increases as areas of authority overlap and the *matrioshka* nesting dolls get smaller and smaller. This is how an *avant-garde* financial daily[5] describes the phenomenon: 'We live in an era of multiple belonging.' In plain English: 'The organisation is buggered.'

There are rules, however, some of them golden. For example, when setting up workplace teams, they must be nominated in such a way as to suggest that they are of vital importance to the business but without going into too much detail (because that would be too much like hard work). The majority of acronyms are therefore permutations of the same words: information, technology, assistance, management, development, application, data, service, executive, centre, network, research, racoon, support, market, product, development, marketing, consumer, customer. (Did you spot the odd one out? You have one minute to find it . . .)

FOREIGN LANGUAGES: *THEY SHALL NOT PASS*

Mongrel business French is crossed with English. Which is surprising, because the French – virtually unanimously – loathe the United States, a country well known for its racism, oppression and vulgarity. In France, thank God, the republican model ensures that the human rights of people of alien origin are explicitly guaranteed – with a vague gesture of self-sacrifice. A free, secular, compulsory education system ensures the triumph of meritocracy. From the time of Montaigne and Racine, the French have been inherently cultivated. A relieved Joe Frenchman can therefore repeat to his heart's content that 'the American model is very different from our own.' Which means, of course: get thee behind me, Satan.

Nevertheless, Joe Frenchman must also recognise – at whatever cost to his self-esteem – that Americans are capitalists *par excellence*. Harvard is money's Bethlehem. We should listen carefully to what Uncle Sam has to say on the subject.

Western European companies suffer from a complex *vis-à-vis* American business schools. As soon as some word catches on in the States, it crosses the Atlantic like a wave and becomes the fashion in our own management schools, business forums and in the mouths of French entrepreneurs. Never mind what's lost in translation; just give a liberal sprinkle to your presentations and your slides – that'll do the trick. Thus *packaging* has replaced *emballage, reporting* has replaced *compte rendu, feedback* has replaced *retour* and *benchmarking* has . . . Actually, I'm not sure what that's replaced. (Do write and tell me if you are clever enough to know the French translation.)

'*Je fais le* follow-up *du* merging project *avec un* coach; *je* check *le* downsizing.' That means: 'Following the merger, a consultant is helping me sack people.'

In the same way, *réengineering* means reorganisation. When a proper French word has developed irrefutably negative connotations, English can provide a very effective euphemism. In the understated world of business, even when things are going badly we must *positiver*. You've been fired? Smile for the camera – say '*fromage*!'

This appalled fascination with the USA goes hand in hand with almost complete ignorance of our cousins across the channel, because nobody in France has ever really mastered their barbarian tongue. Every French employee you ever meet will – shamelessly – lie to you that they are bilingual in English, a stance they can maintain only because the people who hired them speak it just as badly. Nobody is sufficiently competent to test what is, often, only a theoretical ability . . . Let's not complain that the French have little aptitude for the nuances of the language of Shakespeare, a difficult and archaic author. Let's say, rather, the language of Michael Jackson, a singer whose vocabulary expresses less subtlety of whites or greys than the make-up products in his bathroom.

The French manager – supposedly adept in flexible cosmopolitan network communications with the entire universe – is irretrievably bad at languages. Perhaps it's just his petty chauvinist way of fighting globalisation? Perhaps he thinks that, in the future, the business world will speak French – for him (and him alone) the most expressive and elegant language ever to exist. Speaking the no-man's language of business is already hard enough – let's not complicate matters with English too.

PROVERBS, MAXIMS, ADAGES AND AXIOMS

The harvest of maxims and hollow adages nurtured by a delighted business world is staggering. Tired proverbs and shibboleths abound. In fact, only the oldest, most cliché ridden expressions find a home in the comfortingly hackneyed world that is business. There's no room for the vividly old-fashioned – 'the devil take the hindmost' – or the intriguing and edgy – 'what's bred in the bone . . .'. You have to connect – as we say in the office – with the lowest common denominator.

A newcomer to the corporate world is, at first, confused. Then he or she twigs that the apparently impersonal nature of these hand-me-down saws is expressly designed to conceal the concerns and ambitions of the person who uses them. If we were to put together a thesaurus of adages and expressions in current use, the hit parade would be as follows:

'There are no problems, only solutions.' (A ridiculous phrase used by geeks to justify their jobs.)

'Knowledge is power.' (Translation: I know more than you do.)

'Don't work harder, work smarter.' (Motivational phrase used by only the most hypocritical bosses.)

'Everything is a question of organisation.' (As above.)

'I can't bake the bread and grind the flour.' (A proverb expressing the impossibility of doing two things at once. Translation: There is no way I am taking on any more work.)

'Outside the envelope there are no limits.' (Translation: I've had enough of this.)

'There's no smoke without fire.' (Translation: There's something fishy going on here.)

'Let's not beat about the bush.' (Translation: Enough prevarication – let's be frank.')

Meetings are a good place for the connoisseur of meaningless twittering maxims to take notes. And then – incredibly – from the generous belly of the oyster of language, comes a pearl, an amusing, unexpected turn of phrase to reward the countless lost afternoons spent listening to jibberish.

II

THE DICE
ARE LOADED

Your thankless hard work and commitment have been crucial to my career development, Stanzoni. Isn't that the best possible reward for you?

© CartoonStock

PIERO TONIN

IN THE GREAT GAME OF BUSINESS, it's seldom your turn. You are a pawn. Your job is a gift from your company to you. Say thank you to the nice ladies and gentlemen. Be polite and biddable. Don't raise your voice or cause upset. Sit tight and wait for the end of the month. You thought you would have to 'prove yourself', impress people with your 'training' and make yourself 'indispensable' to your employer. Who told you that? You role is to sell and to sell yourself. And not to 'open your big mouth' – as it's called when people lose it in meetings – because that is the best possible invitation for a 'slap'.

MONEY IS TOO DEAR

Everyone works for money and the merry host of objects it can buy. Frédéric Beigbeder hit the nail on the head in his best-seller *99F*:[6] 'He slithers into his mediocre suit, sincerely believing his holding company will collapse without him, climbs into his Mercedes and pumps the accelerator in stationary traffic, a Motorola mobile phone cheeping in the cradle on the dashboard, just above his Blaupunkt car radio . . .'

Money makes up the central nervous system of business, but no one must say so — it's taboo. It's vulgar to mention money: so much better to use refined words such as turnover, results, salary, revenue, budget, bonus and savings. One day I dared to say in the middle of a meeting on motivation that I only came to work to keep the wolf from the door. After fifteen seconds of absolute silence, everyone looked a little pained. Even though the French word for work — *travail* — derives from the Latin *trepalium*, a torture device related to the cross made up of three stakes, you must, in all circumstances, ensure that everyone knows you work 'because you love your work'.

Surely the fact that you chose the job that you do demonstrates that it must be 'fulfilling'? Fulfilling? Who for, exactly? Do you fulfil your job or does your job fulfil you? What a question . . . And don't forget that you didn't choose your work — it chose you. Because what, in the end, are we really at liberty to choose? Our partners? Our religion? Our psychoanalysts? Our lives? Be serious!

We'll have to leave these existential questions to one side. They aren't the issue here (although I'd like the space to pursue them to the point where we ask ourselves what, exactly, it is that we want, which is a very important question indeed). In the end, people work because they have to and no one likes to work. If people liked working, they'd do it for nothing.

Money fascinates people. To prove it, have a look at the

numerous special investigations published by weekly magazines pandering to our unquenchable curiosity about – wait for it – executive salaries. Even though, in France, the range of remuneration is relatively narrow from one business to another, it's always interesting to know how much other people earn. But the money stacking up monthly in your bank account provides, above all, the opportunity to purchase a profusion of diverting gadgets. Having a Palm Pilot, a laptop and a mobile phone can make up for a lot. 'To have or to be' – there's a question. Perhaps, for the middle ranking executive, a more important one than Hamlet's famous 'to be or not to be'. Shakespeare's unhappy hero was, after all, a good deal more miserable than your average manager of today . . . Or was he, I wonder?

'SUCCEED,' THEY TELL YOU . . .

> I'm a success at work all day
> I'm a success in my love affairs
> I frequently change PA
> My office is at the top of the stairs
> I look down to see life unfold
> From here I run my world.

So says the hit song *'The Businessman's Blues'*. But why should he be unhappy, the poor – but filthy rich – devil whose only regret is that he isn't an artist? Perhaps because

the reward for all his scrabbling is derisory, a fact made
more galling by other people's envy. Freud said it: the
engine that drives success, forcing us into conflict with one
another, is no more than a narcissistic quest to assert our
uniqueness, however microscopic the differences.

All this makes status symbols very important in the
business world. Whence the importance of offices which
are assigned according to rank. For example, at rank n
you must put up with a partitioned cubicle measuring
$5.9m^2$ that you share with an intern or a colleague.
Whereas, at rank $n + 1$ you have earned a real office
measuring $6.3m^2$ with – guess what? – a little round table
for meetings. At $n + 2$ your premises benefit from
attractive wooden furniture, absolute incontrovertible
proof that your company loves you more than it does some
of your less favoured colleagues. And that is so important.
Love! Aah . . .

But despite your painstaking climb up through the
ranks and the tangible harvest of gadgets that prove you
have succeeded, the middle manager is destined to remain
a middle manager. Once you become an office guppy – a
bureautier in the term famously coined by the writers of
the film *Le Père noël est une ordure* (*Father Christmas is
Crap!*) – you'll be one for life. The 'senior executive' jobs
(general secretary, president, director, vice-president)
have all been nabbed by *énarques* – graduates in
government from the Ecole Nationale d'Administration.
At the very top you'll find a monopoly of alumni from
exclusive graduate schools such as the Ecole des Mines

and the Inspection des Finances. Just like you, these people are technocrats – but more upmarket. Their careers are woven into France's omnipresent 'network' of power and influence that also includes, for example, 'political decision-makers' (in other words, ministerial offices and party leaderships). The middle manager is middle class through and through – but the senior executive comes from more select stock. There is as much clear, blue water between the boardroom and the mid-ranking executive as there is between the manager and his or her temps or short-term contractors, workers with few rights whom I think of as the 'potentially unemployed'.

You have no one capable of giving you a leg up, no one to put a match to the slumbering rocket in your backside. All you have left is to play a role, to pretend. Whence the importance of clothes in business. They confirm our expectations of our bosses – who are, it goes without saying, fit, sporty, good communicators, enterprising, ambitious and optimistic. They exude a unified aura of relaxed professionalism, emancipated masculinity (or femininity) and stuffy conservatism. The dress code must be respected: in many areas of the economy ladies must wear two-pieces and gents must wear suits. Except for Friday, when we are obliged to 'dress down'. Yes, on Fridays we have the 'right' to wear clothes other than those chosen for the first four days of the week. But Friday gear is only appropriate for Fridays and – surprise, surprise – does not mean clothes that you would choose for yourself, just to relax. No, that would be too easy.

The only real area of choice is ties and socks. And even then . . .

Should we look forward to the added complication of Monday Outfits and Thursday Style. How long will it be before we recreate the court of Louis XIV, with its horde of purposeless aristocrats flapping round the king's skirts, not in order to accomplish anything but just being present?

BALANCE OF POWER: BE CAREFUL, NOW . . .

When you arm-wrestle your company, you lose. In the wild, lions generally beat antelopes. That seems obvious. But that isn't what we are told. Instead we are sold a fictional utopia where all problems are solved by rational negotiation between equal partners and everyone can always win. No one believes this fairy story, especially over pay. Salary levels are determined by a skewed balance of power in a market in which the out-of-work employee stands alone facing a highly organised corporation, capable of taking advantage of every opportunity afforded by labour law.

Businesses use labour law to their own ends. In the OECD countries, they have developed strategies around short-term contracts, temporary staff and flexible hours that undermine aspects of worker protection developed over a century of social upheaval. Thus businesses can 'keep their hands free' and avoid long-term relationships with their staff. This has created a two-tier employment market in France.

On the one hand there are qualified, long-term employees who enjoy reasonably high wages, relative job security, a genuine welfare state and a number of 'perks' (money-off offers, holiday camps for their children, preferential rates, company accommodation etc.). These are the lucky ones – and I am fortunate enough to be one of them. As are you, probably, my dear reader. Otherwise you would likely be doing something other than reading.

On the other hand are the insecure, the freelancers, the contract workers – less well-qualified than the first category, underpaid, poorly protected. Businesses need not offer these short-term drudges either paid leave, health insurance or training. Officially they are responsible for ancilliary services. In fact, they often perform the tasks that the well-off first category people don't want to do. Some must toil so that others may rest.

It's been like this since time immemorial and it isn't about to change. Perhaps this is the only real law on this Earth: for some to be masters, others must be slaves; for some to be rich, others must be poor. And so on. At every opportunity the strong continue to crush the weak, the chiefs to dominate their subordinates. Let's be quite clear – all together now, repeat after me: that's how it is because that's how it is and, in any case, 'there is no alternative'. At least, that's what they would have us believe.

Inside the business world, social injustice can take the form of bullying, the *harcèlement moral* first defined and condemned by French labour law in 2002. The legislation aimed to convict skilfully manipulative bosses – male or female – who treat their secretaries as doormats or abuse their minor executives as nonentities, safe in the knowledge that their defenceless victims will suffer in silence.

True and, at the same time, false. Whatever we do, whatever judicial procedures we put in place, whatever rights are enshrined, most people are unable to assert their sense of self-respect. Perhaps existential angst is fundamental to the human condition. More and more rights, less and less satisfaction. When our parents were young, the Rolling Stones were singing it. It isn't a new idea.

Corporate violence is, therefore, directed at a carefully chosen victim. But where does it come from? From the fact that most middle managers are competing for the same things (a company car, promotion one step up the hierarchy, co-option on to some super-crucial strategic committee). Rivalry rises like a soufflé, intensifies and ends up destabilising the team altogether. Competition only stops generating conflict when a scapegoat is found. This is the view of the philosopher René Girard, who believes that victims are intentionally sacrificed on the altar of solidarity.

Given that we want to promote teamwork among employees, I would like to put forward a mould-breaking idea which torments me every time I attend a boring meeting that goes on a bit too long (often, in other words):

why not make the chief executive the scapegoat? Before 1789, who could have imagined that a king could be guillotined or that the boss could be kidnapped and beheaded? There is an inspirational beauty to French history. Let's honour its memory with a cover of one of its greatest hits. Off with their heads! The sacrifice of a chief executive would give us an opportunity to reconfigure the contract on which the business is based, to rethink relations between senior management and the rest, between the boardroom and the staff, to reassess divisions of labour, offices, salary scales and the rest.

Just imagine the motivational impact of organising such an epic adventure for staff who lack shared goals. Wouldn't it constitute the perfect rebranding exercise for a business caught up in a vicious cycle of abusive bosses and abused employees?

DIPLOMAS AND QUALIFICATIONS – AND HOW TO TURN THEM INTO ORIGAMI CHICKENS

Too many diplomas makes diplomas meaningless. The more there are, the less they are worth. The French national statistical institute estimates that one third of employees are overqualified for the post they hold. Jobs as postal workers, bank tellers and railway conductors generally require a baccalaureate plus three years further education – sufficient paperwork fifty years ago to be considered an intellectual. But this devaluation of certificates and credentials doesn't only apply here.

You want proof that your qualifications no longer mean anything? It doesn't matter what piece of paper serves as a fig leaf to your impotence, your company does no more than tolerate your presence. Take the idea of 'hot-desking' from the oh-so-fertile business environment of the 1980s. This system involves handing out desk space to staff as they arrive each morning for work. The manager without tenure remains 'semi-detached' with no possibility of putting down roots. This pattern reverses our usual understanding. Employees are no longer people employed for their 'usefulness' to the business. It is the business that makes itself useful to the employees by allowing them to work, by granting them the precious boon of employment.

The philosopher Hannah Arendt says that capitalism creates superfluity. It is we, above all, who become superfluous. Indeed, we live in a universe of excess – too much coffee, too much shopping, too many different kinds of bread, too many digital recordings of Beethoven's *Ninth*, too many rear-view mirror options on the latest Renault. Sometimes we think: 'Enough's enough!'

Nevertheless, don't throw out your diplomas quite yet. Despite the fact that they measure neither your intelligence nor your competence, your certificates do prove that you, the worker, the inconsequential executive, are adept at doing as you are told. If you are capable of putting up with a fixed term of study, the stupidity of teachers and the idle chatter and sheep-like instincts of your fellow students, you have clearly also proved that you are capable of enduring thirty years in business, wooden tongue, repetitive chores and all. Because that's what will be expected of you. Most professions today no longer demand high levels of technical or intellectual qualifications because they have, basically, become routine. They require so little initiative or spirit of invention that whoever manages to pass the relevant exams is, *de facto*, overqualified for the majority of available jobs.

It is enough, then, to be mediocre. In the words of Laurent Laurent's satire *Six Months Lost in an Office*: 'Working with a small team of specialists, your role will not be crucial. You will make no operational impact on reorganisation or development. Without a convincing background in economics or finance or significant experience in venture capitalism or mergers and acquisitions (of which you have, besides, never heard), you do not need strong self-motivation in order to promote a long-lasting partnership.'

There is, therefore, room for empty-headed skivers in the five-star universe of major corporations: in business, all are welcome.

EMPLOYMENT AND EMPLOYABILITY – SELLING YOURSELF, PLAYING THE STOOGE

'Our people represent our principal capital.' Could it be that the company that tells us this is lying? Should we be worried that Stalin said the same? Perhaps it means that the more we idealise people, the more in reality they will be oppressed. After all, business hires and fires according to its own needs and unemployment touches all social classes. The bulk of the jobless used to be young people and unskilled workers. Now the list includes skilled workers, foremen, technicians and managers. The French enjoyed thirty years of reassuring upward mobility from 1945 to the 1973 Oil Crisis – *Les Trente glorieuses* – and expected it to continue. Today they have to face up to widespread downward mobility . . . On the other hand, this does demonstrate that things are moving on – which is what you do when your career is over, you 'move on' – just not in the right direction. The moral of this story is that, in business, even when there is nothing to hope for, there are still things to worry about.

Businesses make great demands but promise little, refusing to give long-term commitments. Why would they? Promises – as is well known – are only binding on those who believe them. What's more, in a world where everyone gets the same opportunities, the unemployed have obviously contributed to their own predicament. If they are out of work, it's because they aren't as good as those who do have jobs. If you are made redundant, it's because you didn't manage to make yourself useful or to fulfil your responsibilities or bring in new customers and so on. So there you are, it's your fault! And because it is, quite unequivocally, in the sphere of work that our identities as individuals are formed, you should feel very guilty indeed. 'Work! Work!' Those are your orders. Do any of us retain a vestige of judgement and free will? If so, do we have the right to ask: 'Why?'

To escape from unemployment you must make yourself 'employable'. The potential employee must clothe himself in this indispensable yet poorly defined quality, just like that everyday staple sliced bread, which must be 'toastable' and 'freezable' and – why not? – 'butterable' in order to seduce consumers who seriously couldn't care less. Perhaps we should review the employability of the word 'employ-ability'. All it means is the ability to convince others that you can and should be employed! Why must they be convinced? Because, if everyone is interchangeable and no one indispensable, the middle manager must find ways of making himself stand out from the herd. How? Personality, of course. The golden rule in recruitment these days is that people are hired because of what they are, not because of what they know how to do. 'Interpersonal relations' and 'communication skills' are decisive; knowledge and qualifications are added extras. Soon there will be classes in winning over your interviewer. Welcome to the era of the worthless worker.

So, you have no choice but to be your own sales rep. You must learn to 'sell yourself' as if your personality was a product with a market value. For Tom Peters,[7] the grandiloquent guru of the new economics, success is transforming yourself into a going concern – the brand *You*. The goal is to make it known that you know how to make it known – later on there'll be time to see if you know how to *do* anything. If you just made a bit more effort, you could be like the hero of the film *Jerry Maguire*, played by Tom Cruise, staying up all night writing mission statements and tracts on embracing change, having a web presence for fear of being left behind or reconfiguring such and such an advertising campaign to give it a more fashionable edge.

The image is more important than the product; seduction is more important than manufacturing. The minor executive – hired for his pliability and inconsequence – will make sure it sells. What, exactly? Firstly, standardised, mass-produced goods, generally manufactured in the Third World. Pretty much any Chinese factory worker can do the job. Once made, the less value-added there is invested in the product, the more persuasion must go into convincing the customer to buy it. Secondly, there are goods that are a little harder to produce for which marketing was invented. The purpose of marketing, a discipline with the ethics of the bazaar, is to work out what you do not need and how you might, all the same, be persuaded to buy it. Finally – and above all – there are the services that many people could so easily do without. And here the sales staff really have their work cut out to prevent the customers realising that what they are actually buying is so much hot air . . .

There are moves towards giving a personalised service and paying attention to individual customer needs, but these are solely designed to reintroduce made-to-measure values in a capitalist production line that has completely eliminated them. This is the 'little extra', the 'personal touch' that is so lacking in a homogenised universe. Businesses ape the authentic values that the steamroller of mass production has done so much to destroy and charge their executives with promoting these fantasies.

That's what we are for, that's our job. It's so that we can be our company's stooges that they gave us those qualifications — and, tangentially, because we are intelligent. (It does sometimes happen, but only by accident.)

WORDS DEFEATED

There are fewer and fewer labour conflicts. The number of days lost to strikes is going down. Order reigns in our workplaces, in factories and open-plan offices and on the piazza at La Défense. More to the point, how can you rise up against unassailable arguments such as 'modernity' and 'autonomy', 'openness' and 'sociability'? How do you oppose authorities and institutions who endlessly repeat that they are 'taking account of changed circumstances' the better to meet 'the expectations of society' and 'the needs of individuals'?

In theory, everyone can speak their mind. The boss's door is always open; anyone can go and have a chat. And you say '*tu*' to each other, not '*vous*'. And the boss takes on the role of sympathetic facilitator, friend, therapist even. Once or twice a year each employee conducts their own 'annual performance review' and ends up with 'an overall verdict'. Workers are given the right to express judgements on themselves and on others – but how, then, can we expect them to unite in shared opposition to their bosses? Certainly they have free speech, but that's as far as it goes. Speech leads to nothing. Talk to the hand. What you say and what you think are of no importance. 'Words, words, words,' whispered the pop singer Dalida back in the 1970s in a memorable duet with the gorgeous Alain Delon . . .

Nothing has changed in France since the reign of Louis XIV: authority is exercised in the most centralised way possible. Decisions are rarely taken collectively. Businesses loathe face-to-face negotiations. They avoid discussions in the presence of all parties to a disagreement that might lead to compromise. And, of course, the wooden tongue argument is a one-way street. By replacing and discrediting normal language, it denies any form of answer. Communication is short-circuited and the employee is struck by aphasia. If there ever was a genuine public reassessment, don't you think people would see that the traditional French values of good taste, proportion and balance have been turned upside down?

Decisions are handed down from on high and the powers-that-be are structured in such a way that it is almost impossible to see where they really come from. Which makes it difficult to know who to tell that you disagree. Who decided this? No one knows. Is there an inspired and benevolent Other who will take decisions in favour of the public good? No, but many people think there is, which gives the idea substance. And, thanks to this hypothetical being, we relinquish our prerogatives as responsible employees. Great Other, who art on high, let thy will be done . . .

Because the use of particular words has consequences and engages no responsibilities, all that remains is the banal pleasure of using them to criticise colleagues. Spurred on by petty rivalries, many people take great satisfaction in slagging off their workmates and – *sotto voce* – the company. As General de Gaulle said, unhappy employees easily fall prey to belligerence, intolerance and petulance. This swiftly develops into a uniquely French condition: *le tracassin*, a word made up by the General based on the word *tracas* – hassle – and meaning the inability to keep oneself to oneself, being a stirrer.

Confronted with the bankruptcy of language, what do the unions do? (Their role is, after all, to put these things right.) Although well established in major companies and – above all – in the public sector, they aren't so much caught offside as sidestepped. Which is no surprise. The new neo-management deal has them baffled. They barely have a role because they are considered dinosaurs from a hierarchical, bureaucratic world whose time has passed, yet somehow they cling determinedly on. And, of course, union leaders are all people who rebelled in May 1968 and, if they'd managed to change anything then, we would have noticed by now. As a result, trade unionists are often disillusioned fifty-somethings bristling with contempt for the inertia and lack of 'spirit' in the young.

Even though the trade unions seem a little behind the times, undermined by an inexorable erosion of their membership, they sometimes play a vital role when a conflict becomes a stand-off. The unforgettable strikes of 1995 when, for several weeks, the major French cities were brought to a standstill, are sufficient reminder. It is amusing that most Parisians look back with affection on that immense citywide traffic jam which turned every journey into an interminable nightmare. Some of them, it is true, took advantage of the lack of tube trains to harpoon an attractive hitchhiker or two. Others took the time to chat to other people. In fact, pretty much everyone started talking – in the streets, in the cafés, everywhere! Actually, it was brilliant. When will we talk to one another like that again?

OF THE WORKER'S IMMINENT OBSOLESCENCE

What does business believe in? Innovation. Innovation is always right. Hiring someone young – an infusion of new blood – is quite naturally a precious objective in a company panicking at the idea that it might be out of touch. Look around you. Society incessantly offers us ubiquitous model images of perpetually fresh individuals in blooming good health achieving great things in every area of life.

The 'kid' has no love handles and can wear a suit and tie without displaying unpleasant rolls of flab. He arrives in the world of work naively sure of himself. He thinks that the words 'proactive' and 'benchmarking' actually mean something. He believes that the sacrosanct injunction to be 'autonomous' should be taken literally. He thinks his qualities will be recognised and is convinced he will be . . . loved. Oh tender youth! The 'kid' is particularly precious in that the company has contradictory expectations: that he should keep quiet but also argue, learn but also suggest, keep in step and make himself stand out . . . It's a little like a child within its family. The family want their little darling to respect and resemble its parents but, at the same time, it hopes that the child succeeds where the mother and father have failed. The two outlooks are completely incompatible!

'Seniors' are another kettle of fish. Historically, lay-offs and redundancy schemes started by deciding that employees over fifty were no longer 'employable' (see above: *Employment and employability*). In your fifties? Get out!

In the 1970s and 1980s, the cleansing of seniors was made easier by a system of early retirement and lump sum payments, financed by the public purse. Thank you, the Nation. You might well ask if it is legitimate to pay taxes to subsidise jettisoning people in the prime of life . . . Today, in France, the result is that only one third of men between 55 and 64 work — a world record. We must recognise that the exclusion of 'older' workers is a clever way to minimise disputes. Fifty-year-olds are less pliable than thirty-somethings flushed with achieving their first

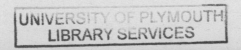

stable job, who have swallowed the fiction that they were oh-so-very lucky to get through the company's audition process to play such a central role.

To sum up, you are finished at an age where, in politics, you are considered a spring chicken or a young Turk (although not in France where young Turks are not appreciated). Finished at the same age as Cézanne painted his splendid Sainte-Victoire series or Dostoievski wrote *The Brothers Karamazov*. To use an expression beloved of consultants but generally applied to products – the executive's 'life cycle' is short. From the 'rise to power' (up to 30 years old and sometimes more) to the decline (45 onwards) is but a single step. A stroke of a pen – in the human resources department – leads from the Capitol and its seat of power to the executioner on the Tarpeian Rock.

But the rapid obsolescence of the workforce cannot continue forever. The shared desire of businesses and individual workers to see early retirement flatly contradicts the requirements of an ageing society with fewer and fewer young people to pay for the seniors' pensions. The issue is a powder keg and its repeated explosions make for diverting viewing for the entomologist or the city-dweller. The multiple strikes of May and June 2003 over – among other things – the state pension scheme were proof enough. Still, at least there was something going on. And France, shaken by these exhilarating conflicts, appeared suddenly, well, younger.

III
THE FINEST CON-TRICKS

'We must lighten the load . . . you're a good company man, aren't you, Carruthers?'

MANAGER OR EMPLOYEE, they tell you lies. Don't listen. The company spins tall stories, traps for the unwary. Let's steal the bait together. Compulsory mobility and the constant droning discourse on ethics, flexibility and new information and communications technologies are porky pies.

MOVING ON – GOING NOWHERE

Moving on is the hint of the Infinite offered to middle managers; the only hint within their reach. At a time when society itself has lost direction, workers are being asked to 'imagine themselves a bright future'. Do you feel you are living the life of a mercenary, paid to espouse causes not your own, despatched into environments you feel are alien? Never mind. 'Be a vector for your own development,' sing the siren voices. Moving on has become the categorical imperative for a mode of capitalism whose final purpose – hurry up now – is to sell worthless yet indispensable ersatz products.

In his untranslated novel *La Boîte* – a word meaning both *company* and *box* – François Salvaing gives us a typical dialogue between boss and employee:

'How do you see your career developing?' asked William Lévêque, the new HR director, fresh in from the automotive industry.

'Three years in each post.'

'Why?'

'Any longer and you get stuck and other people think you're a fossil. Any less and you don't really get to the bottom of things. You don't see the wood for the trees.'

Move on! Three years at HQ, two years in Singapore running a subsidiary, three years in Piddletrenthide doing a management audit. Your court will follow in your train. In homage to the great god 'mobility', your children and your wife (or husband) are expected to move house too, leaving behind their daily routines, their work and their friends with a smile on their faces and standing politely to attention as they do so. And if, by some extraordinary hazard, your train will not follow . . . change your wife (or husband). He or she is insufficiently mobile to follow your vapour trail. We have the example – writ large – of senior executives, high-tech nomads shuttling between major national and multinational boardrooms, staying only a few years in each post, collecting bonuses, golden hellos and golden goodbyes worth millions of euros as they go.

There's the proof. Everything's for sale, including human beings. The writings of the Marquis de Sade imagined a sexual utopia in which everyone had the right to enjoy everybody else – human beings reduced to their sexual organs, completely anonymous and interchangeable. Of course, Donatien-Alphonse-François de Sade was a depraved aristocrat, the last of his line. But today, every one of us has become a commercial product, destined to be bought and sold as and when required by business. Because, for a company, the human being is such a bore – blinkered by experience, bowed down by training, worn out by repetition, depressed by the surrounding culture or climate. The human loaf is so indigestible! It creates a barrier to the policy of non-stop mobility they are trying to impose on everybody.

The typical middle-ranking executive also gets in the way. He isn't at all flexible. He is frightened of being knocked from his lofty perch, forced to take on some task that he considers beneath him. France is still basically feudal, harking back to a time when your station in society was fixed for life. It is a country where anyone lucky enough to have an acre to till defends it tooth and nail. The obsession with rank, privileges and prerogatives is the motivation for much corporate behaviour – the arrogance of caste, endless struggles over precedence. They all drain the staff's energy and make them less pliable . . .

The average executive isn't any more mobile in the geographical sense either. He doesn't dream of moving house every three years. His vision is to buy a bungalow in some residential suburb of Paris, firstly in aspirational

Chaville, then later, as he climbs the social ladder, in plush Vésinet, for him the ultimate badge of success. Once he's taken on twenty years of debt to acquire his 'that'll-do-me', there's no way he'll want to move.

By happy chance, he lives near La Défense, a hideous, soulless business district straight out of Aldous Huxley's *Brave New World*. Here our service sector slave can be 'mobile' without moving house, because La Défense overflows with 'job opportunities'. If luckier still, he might be able to limit his mobility to changing skyscraper or just changing floors. He could start his career on the seventh floor of the Gan Tower, move up to the twenty-fifth, then get transferred to the thirty-second floor of the Ariane, then back to HQ on the twenty-fifth of the Gan before toddling off into a well-earned retirement.

Moving on can be so tiring!

BUSINESS CULTURE: CULTURE MY ARSE!

The word 'culture' infiltrated the business world about twenty years ago. In his untranslated *Extension du domaine de la lutte* – enlargement of the field of struggle – Michel Houellebecq writes ironically: 'Well before the word became fashionable, my company developed an authentic business culture (it created a logo, gave the employees company sweatshirts, ran workshops on motivation in Turkey). It's a profitable business with an enviable reputation in its area – in every way a *good place to work.*'

By definition, culture has no useful purpose – but as 'business culture' it is being forced to work. Straightaway you can see the catch. There is nothing more contemptuous of culture than business. 'Business culture' is an oxymoron, a figure of speech composed of concepts whose meanings are at odds with one another. The idea of a special culture seems very useful to management when everything is going well, because it creates an artificial sense of identity and belonging. But, when things go badly, people decide it's an out of date obstacle to change.

In fact, 'business culture' is no more than the momentary crystallisation of a given group of people's current stupidity. This micro-patriotism is comprised of a compacted mass of stale routines – all paths of least resistance – and patterns of dress and behaviour that tip over into self-parody. Rewritten by management, it becomes the official history, complete with heroes and feast days, designed to motivate and foster identification with a united, unified team. It is expressed through a glut of meaningless seminars, unwearable T-shirts and badges – yes, badges! – with so-called motivational slogans. These catastrophically hard-to-swallow initiatives are to the business world what busts of Marianne and statues of Joan of Arc – those unimpeachable invocations to sacrosanct 'republican values' – are to France.

Why so many knick-knacks and watchwords? Because, like society as a whole, businesses are threatened with disintegration. The fundamental issue for today's communities, nations or companies is 'how to live together'. And we are finding fewer and fewer answers. It is precisely this issue that exhausts prominent contemporary thinkers such as Jürgen Habermas or John Rawls. And given that business has no more idea than the wider community how to pull people together, it artificially creates a 'family' by setting up icons that the employees can – supposedly – identify with.

Let's leave them to it. The day when firms no longer have any other objective than to create symbols for their staff to identify with will be the day we know that companies are irretrievably doomed to disappear. In the meantime, we have somehow to find the will-power to get up each morning for something that, in reality, means nothing at all – and it ain't easy.

ETHICS: WHERE'S THE OPPOSITION?

The dominant tone of current debate is right thinking, morally irreproachable and ecologically correct. The business world couldn't hope to escape the frenzied escalation of sympathy and understanding, the tidal wave of non-specific charity, compulsory idealism, unquestioning solidarity and universal human rights crawling out from under every stone. So business adopted the freshly imported American concept of ethics, which is to morality what chicory is to coffee. Ethics has invaded the business world, with its mission statements and policies[8] that attempt confusedly to define, at one and the same time, general principles, values and detailed rules of behaviour. Ethics cleans consciences whiter than white without scrubbing.

The new ethics cliché comes in different forms. There is the fantasy of 'business as citizen' or of 'sustainable development'. There's a whiff of oxymoron about both (I've already defined the term in the earlier section *Business culture*). And whether or not there's a contradiction in terms, what firm today is not 'concerned' by the greenhouse effect and the holes in the ozone layer? The problem is that ethics is a little like culture: the less you have, the thinner you spread it. And talking about it too much is suspicious – do we protest too much . . . ? Besides, in the oil industry, Shell is in top spot on the 'ethically correct' chart. Enlightened, Shell? I'm not so sure, but at the headquarters of Europe's most profitable conglomerate there is a conviction that morality pays. Beware the wolf in sheep's clothing . . .

Ethics proves that businesses turn everything to their financial advantage, even things inimical to profit, ethics first and foremost. While businesses absorb and deform everything within reach, their behaviour – their business 'values' – seep out like an oil spill spreading its black stain. Public hospitals have been infected by the managerial virus, making every effort to employ the appropriate vocabulary – 'niche', 'reserves of productivity', 'customers'. Schools too. The 'action plans' of educational organisations now include 'skills balance sheets', bringing us nicely on to 'target setting contracts'

with pupils. The productive logic of business has become
the key benchmark for a society whose very speech and
dreams have become contaminated by marketing.

The proof? The immoderate use of the verb 'to manage'.
In business language, it means organising people and
things, but it has crept into every sphere of existence: the
socialists manage their defeat, a woman her divorce, a
sportsman his injuries, an Olympic medallist her success,
a doctor her patients – and we each manage our sex lives.

'Hi-ho, hi-ho, it's off to manage we go . . .'

STRATEGY: OR GIVING AN IMPRESSION OF INTELLIGENCE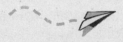

Strategy – out it pops! Just saying it out loud makes you
feel you are entering the holy of holies. The word – which
has no precise meaning – comes from military usage where
it refers to 'tactics' but on a broader scale. Following a deep
examination of the question, I am in a position to confirm
that there are only two available strategies: refocusing on
core activities (understood to mean 'what the business is
good at') and diversification (things the business isn't good
at but will not hesitate to learn because 'you shouldn't
have all your eggs in one basket'). Given that there are only
two possible choices, strategy is easy. I refer here to the
words of the Cuban *líder maximo*, Fidel Castro, in one of
his draining, rolling-river speeches from the great days of
yore (some time ago now): 'There is no third way.'

Let's move on to strategy's second lesson. When companies diversify, it is always justified by synergies between the 'core business' and the new activities. Synergies between two disparate trades are like the intertwined hearts of a couple in love. Reasons — usually completely irrational ones — are given *in hindsight* for bringing the two people or activities together. Strategy is as much based on hunches and intuition as fortune telling. Scott Adams makes fierce fun of the concept: 'What is our strategy? Our business strategy can be defined as follows: we place all our existing ideas — in other words any ideas at all — in a mixing bowl. We add all our competitors' good ideas. We stir.'[9]

The good thing about strategy is that it allows you to produce reams of tasty documentation in office newspeak. In the French energy company I work for, I recently read a bravura performance from a firm of consultants: 'Remaining leader requires secure sourcing and/or positioning the group on midstream gas, as well as identifying an optimal mass market production portfolio/mix. This takes us away from the pure player model on which our offer package was based. Interdivisional internal corporate leadership vectors must show determination, taking account of bottom-up feedback. Prevent-ive maintenance time must be factored into gaps between the consolidated vision and the 2006 objectives.' Now there's a mouthful . . .

Reading rubbish like this proves that the people who write strategies are no more intelligent than you are. Who does write them, then? They are either drawn up by a learned assembly of parasites (advisers, right-hand men, consultants) or by the boss all alone. The first solution – though not a good one – is better than the second, for it does sometimes avoid the biggest blunders. And we have so many fine examples of gigantic blunders in France that you start to think we must be cursed. In 1992, the Crédit Lyonnais almost went bankrupt due to an ill-judged expansion plan that was designed to make it the biggest bank on the planet. Ten years later, here we go again: in 2002, the financial crisis at Vivendi finally dispersed the mirage of a new economics and drew a line under the company's attempt to become the global media and communications number two.

Both the failed bosses – Jean-Yves Haberer and Jean-Marie Messier – are oh-so-chic Inspectors of Finance graduates from the best colleges in France and Navarre. In both cases, too, the idea of buying a Hollywood studio – MGM for one and Universal for the other – was sold as clever diversification. You see, banks and recycling plants are so mundane, so yucky! But Hollywood turned out to be central to their problems. Messier was discovered to be a Haberer clone, making exactly the same mistakes and failing in exactly the same way. (The business world is desperately short of glamour. All things considered, it isn't surprising they dreamt of paste jewellery and sequins. It could desperately do with some.)

But the litany of French catastrophes on American soil is not over. At the end of 2003, the most recent example was the Executive Life affair, which will – surprise,

surprise – cost French taxpayers a small fortune. It all began with the mad story of the 1991 acquisition of a Californian life insurance company by a Crédit Lyonnais subsidiary. They were innocent days when money flowed like water and the Frenchies thought they were making the deal of the century. Unfortunately, it was illegal. As well as becoming an affair of state, it turned into a devilishly complex issue in law, training media spotlights on the dubious hand-in-hand relationship between French industry and government. Nevertheless, there will be no trial because in our great country we do not like to wash our dirty linen in public. The slate will be wiped clean by paying the Americans a fine of $770 million. This agreement leaves Jean Peyrelevade, chief executive of Crédit Lyonnais at the time of the road crash, sprawled at the side of the road with a handful of other compromised directors. It does, however, bring comfort to the current owner of Executive Life, the businessman François Pinault, a friend of Jacques Chirac.

For a few enlightened zealots, strategy is a kind of magic wand, capable of transforming a frog into a prince – or could it be the other way round?

INFORMATION AND COMMUNICATIONS TECHNOLOGIES ARE THE FUTURE!

IT is the future. I heard this said for the first time when I was at secondary school in the 1970s. ICTs are the offspring of computers and the internet. For two decades businesses have been investing hand over fist in these technologies, hoping for phenomenal productivity gains. Now, computers are everywhere; the internet will change our world, create jobs and herald a strong period of growth. With the internet, all our problems will be solved. The internet will revolutionise the history of humankind. This wonderful communications tool will eradicate problems caused by frontiers, by race and religion. The internet will bring freedom to remote rural areas, reduce ghettoisation, promote trade between the developed and the developing world, educate the illiterate and young children, liberate housewives. It will make us all brothers. There will be no more war. All together now, sing after me: 'All you need is the internet, la-la-la-la-la!'

The siren song is seductive; reality is less kind. For the time being, the only undeniable impact of the IT spring clean has been to make vast numbers of otherwise very useful secretaries redundant. Anything else? No. The influential Nobel Prize-winning economist Robert Solow suggests that if new technologies have increased productivity, it is in the ICT sector that they have done it.

Is that it? Seriously, doesn't it beggar belief?

Despite failing to demonstrate any economic usefulness, ICT has at least spawned its own language, and that shouldn't be underestimated.

The language of ICT is abstruse. Only fully initiated members of the web tribe can understand its discussions of disparate development platforms, the choice of the most appropriate software solutions, all couched in terms of html, xml, Dreamweaver and Coldfusion. A friend of mine who understands all this sent me an example: 'The merging of WSFL and XLang is at least as important as the two new protocols themselves. The major interest for web service providers either side of the firewall is embodied by the rapid development of *ad hoc* xml applications. BPEL4WS will provide a more standardised method to achieve this by simply merging two established languages. But it appears that various operational protocols from the B2B interface have been neglected in the development work, notably the ebXML protocol, the Business Process Modelling Langue (BPML) and the brand new Web Services Choreography Interface (WSCI).'

I notice some of my readers have dropped off . . .

What's it all about? Reading sentences like these, we feel stupid – and that's probably the point of them. They highlight our inferiority. It's incomprehensible and it is, at the same time, incomprehensible that it should be incomprehensible because we know about the internet! We spend hours at work surfing for essential factoids about the seawater temperature in the Maldives or fly-fishing on the Dordogne.

IV
YOUR COLLEAGUES ARE MORONS

'Excellent, Simmons! I admire a yes-man
who's not afraid to say yes.'

BECAUSE I DON'T WANT TO FALL OUT with my colleagues, this chapter needs a health warning. I am reminded of the words of the well-known editor and wine-lover, Françoise Verny — who, few people know, spent 15 years earning a crust with Kodak (find out more in her autobiography, *Le Plus Beau Métier du Monde* — the best job in the world). She says that you meet just as many — or just as few — good people in business as elsewhere. I have found this to be true. Therefore, in this chapter, I will be holding up to ridicule only certain archetypes and caricatures that otherwise we wouldn't bother with.

THE STANDARD MODEL EXECUTIVE:
FRENCHIFIED, SMOOTH, PREFERABLY MALE

Middle ranking executives constitute a substantial proportion of the very average French citizen so vividly described by Pierre Dac: 'The average Frenchman is an invertebrate mammal. He has the distinction of presenting no distinctive features whatsoever. He believes, above all, in officially endorsed law and order. Generally speaking, his identity papers describe him as follows: Height – average; Hair line – average; Colour of eyes – uncertain; Nose – average; Jaw line – oval; Distinguishing marks – none.' To sum up, the Frenchman summoned to the ranks of middle management is a production line unit and he looks exactly like everyone else.

Why such uniformity? To start with, because certain structures inevitably attract a certain sort of person. Also because business is, quintessentially, a place of exclusion, an environment in which anyone at all out of the ordinary is, at best, only tolerated. In this way, businesses reproduce the same blockages that afflict the society they belong to. The rigidity of French society breeds arthritic companies because the selection process for new employees no longer functions properly. The number of candidates putting themselves up for tests for a given post is completely out of proportion to the number of people likely to succeed. Because companies are swimming in CVs and because 'there isn't a job for everybody', they have to make a choice. And they always choose the same sort of people.

It is not my intention to march beneath the sickly-sweet banner of 'United Colours' imperialism, but let's face facts: if the candidate is the wrong age, nationality or gender, rejection is without right of appeal. The same goes for health problems or certain disqualifying life paths which a CV cannot fully disguise. Disabled? Yes, we recognise your right to work, but somewhere else, for a different company. You've spent a few years in prison? Finding work will be very difficult indeed. The French acclaim Victor Hugo's well-known novel *Les Misérables*, but no one wants to give Jean Valjean – its big-hearted ex-convict hero – a job.

Blacks, Arabs, foreigners and 'young people from ethnic backgrounds' – as they are euphemistically called – find it even harder. They are rare indeed at executive level. And it isn't just because they are so much more talented at football or show business. The absence of relevant data – it is illegal in France to use ethnic origin or religion in database fields – makes proper debate impossible. Everyone knows there is a problem but it's tucked away out of sight. As for homosexuals, even though these 'sensitive young men' are welcome in professions involving creativity or fashion, the consensus is that they don't exist in industry. Perversely, in industry, homosexuality just isn't fashionable. The result of this ambient homophobia is that, faced with a choice between equally competent candidates, gays have little chance of making it to the boardroom.

Some are more equal than others at work, and women are less equal than many. Women earn less money than men with equivalent responsibilities and find it difficult to obtain senior positions. Why? Simply because they are not often seen after six or seven o'clock in the evening. They are, therefore, not available at those strategic moments when the company closes ranks and tots up the names of those whose devotion is unconditional. Perhaps it's no surprise that studies show that women's professional development is handicapped by family life, but they also show that men's careers are given a boost. How's that? It's just too bad for the mother who does her job better and more efficiently than others – which is, in my experience, often the case – she isn't the one who writes the rules. Men do.

It's well known that men spend more time at work than their female colleagues. Some say this is because their instincts as predators are never fully satisfied. Others maintain that it's because of their laid-back attitude towards trivial household chores. In France, men undertake just 20 per cent of cooking and cleaning, an amount that, I'm sure you'll agree, shouldn't overtax the poor dears. Because women toil far harder at home than men, they are twice as likely to work only part time, feeding more inequality into the system and reinforcing the glass ceiling that separates them from power. As a consequence, in the upper financial stratosphere – in other words, among the dynamic battalions of senior executives – women make up just 5 per cent. Statistics don't always deceive – these are overwhelming.

So, equality is just a distant dream. It's tempting to bang your fist on the table and demand that businesses appoint quotas of women executive directors, but would that actually achieve anything? A recent French law has imposed percentages of women in politics, but the major political parties prefer to pay the fines rather than putting members of the fairer sex on their electoral lists.

Fortunately we can console ourselves with the knowledge that women live longer than men and that men are four times more likely to kill themselves. This kind of inequality is intolerable but it is, at least, a kind of justice!

THE *MANAGER* – FRENCH STYLE: SO LIGHTWEIGHT HE'S HOLLOW

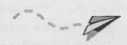

The old-school executive, with his faint fragrance of hierarchy and status, is no more. In fact, the word 'manager' has lost all meaning, except perhaps that he or she has been to university and can't be asked to sweep the floor. At least in big companies they can't; small companies don't stand on ceremony. I've known people with five years of higher education instructed to open parcels or lay cables in the floor void (supported by a properly qualified technician, of course!) No, 'executive' is a title not a job. But still, it's better to be one than not. In business, everyone spends their days doing the work of their immediate superior. The higher you go, the less you have to do. The more important you become, the less you graft. This is one of the immutable laws of the world of work. That said, it's not good to be too high up either, spending every minute on display. No one is happier twiddling their thumbs than a politician – but in the glare of the public gaze everything changes. You have to enjoy that. For me, having nothing to do, I'd rather stay at home. I know I'll never amount to anything, but – hey-ho!

The French word for manager is *cadre* but because, generally speaking, managers don't manage, in France the person who does the job of the *cadre* is designated by the English word *manager*. This Frenchified *manager* is a relatively recent invention. It became popular and established its meaning in the 1980s. At the same period, the tired French concept of *gestion* (meaning, of course, management) was refreshed by renaming it *management*! *Manager* modernises the role of the *cadre* in the same way. Different words don't make these tasks any more exciting, but updating the terminology gives it more bite. You see in business, like anywhere else, words get worn out.

So what does this *manager* do? Of course, he is fluent in office-speak, but that's not all. He is also a 'team leader', a 'catalyst' and a 'visionary'. He must – dare I say it? – 'breathe life' into the business. He doesn't provide, he inspires. He doesn't try to accumulate a fortune or build an empire. His raw materials are people not things. Rather than confront a practical task or develop a solution for a problem, he must tackle People. The authority he acquires over his team grows out of the 'confidence' he inspires in them, thanks to his 'communication' and 'listening' skills, demonstrated in his dealings with others. Youthful, cheerful and attractive, our *manager* must maintain the illusion that he is free to choose, to create even. Which calls to mind what one of the Bolshevik leaders said: 'Being a Marxist means being creative.' It's the same in the business world. You really can't deny that there is some common ground between the Soviet Union and the much cosier universe of our major competitive capitalist companies.

In extreme cases the *manager* pretends he is an artist or – let's not mince our words – an intellectual. In the days when Jean-Marie Messier (see below: *Those you will never meet*) was the darling of the media and a certain intelligentsia, the writer Philippe Sollers, who clearly doesn't know how to take a backward step, didn't hesitate to open a dialogue with the messiah of the new economics. This collector's piece was published in his review *L'Infini* – the infinite – and showed us the two of them duelling with buttoned foils to see who could be the more subversive . . . A sonic boom was soon heard as both quickly broke the moron barrier.

The modern *manager* is free of the burden of possessions and the restrictions of hierarchy. He is open to new ideas and believes in nothing. Unlike the Soviet New Man, no cause attracts his allegiance. He feels no loyalty towards the company he works for. He isn't very interested in work well done because, at bottom, his sense of success has been hollowed out. On this point as well as many others, René-Victor Pilhes, the *avant-garde* author of the novel *L'Imprécateur* – the spell-caster[10] – can help us out: 'An executive is neither a financier, a technician or a trader. I suppose he organises pretty much everything . . . The executive path leads to what is called *management*. *Management* is the process of removing all emotional factors from plans, figures, organisations and transactions – in fact from all possible decisions. This is why, for a great *manager*, there are no differences between religions, between political regimes, between unions etc.'

The devil take those who make judgements, who have preferences, who spend their lives doing just one thing! In theory, pride and the profit motive drive the world of trade, but these characteristics aren't welcome in the volatile, fluid world championed by business. Appearances are more important than the quality of the work done. Reputations and who gets the credit count for more than any real accomplishments. From heavy industry to virtual world, from bronze work to paperwork – perhaps, in a single phrase, that is the complete history of capitalism!

THE MANAGER AND CULTURE: AN UNLIKELY COUPLE

What does a manager know how to do? Nothing in particular, as it happens. He's a generalist. He understands 'overall issues'. Well, he understands some of them and then only from a distance. He studied at the classic colleges of the French Ivy League – schools of politics, certain business schools. He didn't learn much, but he learned how to get selected. He reads the editorials of two or three writers, experts in accepted wisdom and cliché. He spices up his vocabulary with simple English or American terminology and makes a big old noise about it all. Our man – or woman – never looks deeply into things because there's no point in drowning yourself in facts and figures. It doesn't clarify matters; on the contrary, it makes them more complex. No, don't explore issues. 'Happily our firms are not in the hands of intellectuals. If they were, what would become of our consumer society?' cries one of René-Victor Pilhes' characters in *L'Imprécateur*.

Let's be clear, the standard issue manager is an ignoramus. This shouldn't surprise us because the intellectual world he inhabits is completely deficient. For him, culture is a kind of gadget that he can employ in order to shine at the dinner table. It is unfortunate that a top-of-the-range BMW and a gold watch bracelet can sometimes come across as vulgar, whereas an apposite quotation – well, that's another story.

Business has understood that culture can sometimes provide a useful counterpoint to the decisions the senior executives are handing down – a little soul, an unexpected breadth of understanding. So companies are prepared to spend impressive sums on training their most brilliant executives in order to safeguard the smooth functioning of the economy. They hire top-ranking university professors who are delighted to earn much more than they would in higher education, cutting down the great classics of our wonderful artistic tradition, reducing to bite-sized 'digests' an extensive cultural heritage once the preserve of a leisured elite who read books and listened to music for pleasure . . . No, I don't believe it, surely not . . . Yes, really, for pleasure.

You see, our highest-flying executives have never found

the time to read Michel Foucault, to listen to a Mozart opera or to see a Fellini film. They are far, far too busy, I'm afraid. Busy? What with? Busy with their diaries, that's what. And what fills their diaries? Meetings. Meetings for what purpose? To organise work – their own work and other people's. Is that really more useful than to read a novel in which you learn a good deal about your fellow men, about their natures and ambitions – and the limits to their ambitions – Balzac's *The Human Comedy*, for example? It's worth asking . . .

And this is why our *managers* are all of the species *homo economicus moronus*, the most common and the most complete form of New Man – created by business.

GEEKS VERSUS SALES REPS: SCORE DRAW

Given the vast quantities of paperwork it produces, you might think that business needed people capable of writing a sentence that includes a subject, an object and a verb. Curiously, this is not the case. Business is not fond of those people it sneeringly calls 'literary'. They 'don't know how to do anything'. They are 'dreamers'. The geek, on the other hand, knows how to do things. He has studied maths. And maths, as everyone knows, is the rational science *par excellence*.

The geek is a pragmatist. He tries to get at the heart of things without complicating his life. He is wary of man – warier still of woman – because people are, by their very nature, unreliable, an endless source of nuisance. The geek's dream is total automation to the 'nth degree', in 'real time', controlled by machines which work in such a way that all he needs to do is press a button to achieve a result. The geek is, necessarily, a misfit. So he often appears funny – unintentionally. His maladjusted side would make him an amusing canteen buddy if he weren't so tedious.

The geek recognises that life does not yet function like a well-oiled machine. In the meantime, he enjoys solving problems and, when there aren't any problems to solve, he makes some up. This explains why he's always busy with something completely useless. Well done the geek! Unfortunately, as a counterweight to the influence of the geeks, the business also hires sales reps, often pretentious morons convinced that everything can be bought or sold. No surprise, then, that skirmishes between the two castes are frequent. When the geeks are in charge, the sales staff is tasked with promoting and commercialising the rational solutions devised by the technicians. But how difficult is that? Consider Concorde and the Superphénix nuclear power station, technological luxury items and money pits. On the other hand, when the sales reps hold the tiller, cost reduction becomes the cry as they hack away with their machetes at the superfluous but sometimes amusing activities dreamt up by the inventive geeks.

The technicians and the bean counters pull big business in opposite directions, in control of one leg each. No wonder it often falls flat on its face.

CONSULTANTS: NO ONE LIKES
TO BE TAKEN FOR A FOOL

These days, it is unthinkable that someone might bring up a child without the assistance of a psychologist for his Oedipus complex, an orthophonist to teach him to read and additional tutoring to help him absorb the drivel they pour into him at school. The world we live in is characterised by relentless support. It makes you wonder how, exactly, without shrinks and paramedical care paid for by national insurance contributions, humanity ever managed to invent printing or build cathedrals. (The mystery is such that it lends credence to the sincerely held thesis that the pyramids and other pharaonic buildings must have been built by extra-terrestrials.)

It's the same in business. Because, these days, organisations are supposed to be 'adaptive' and individuals 'creative', everyone needs help in bringing forth new knowledge and ideas. Of this need a new and indispensable profession was born: the *coach*.

The *coach*'s role is to provide personalised assistance designed to help individuals achieve their full potential. Today's organisations make demands on the full range of our abilities. It is at last possible for us properly to thrive. The *coach*'s job is to nurture the seeds of this potential to fruition.

Actually, a *coach* is just a consultant with a touch of rebranding to give it a more 'with it' feel . . . and to pick up the baton of society's strongly-felt desire for self-fulfilment and freedom. You see, neo-management strategies supposedly offer each one of us the liberty to be no longer a mere instrument, to achieve instead personal satisfaction through the realisation of our most heartfelt ambitions.[11] But this so-called liberty is, to business, what pornography is to sexual freedom: a paltry satisfaction. To paraphrase the comedian Cabu who used the English words in italics in his French stand-up routine: 'I've been doing some *coaching*, some *team-building* and some *e-learning* . . . and I'm still *merde-ing* bored!'

The *coach* isn't the only blood-sucking parasite at work. Businesses spend millions on an array of 'specialist' auditors and consultants who are paid for telling their employers what they want to hear and confirming the decision-makers in their powerful hunches. The consultants' strategic and organisational visions must be presented in the form of austere and often unreadable documents, containing a long list of 'items', reinforced by schematic illustrations composed of geometrical shapes and arrows symbolising the numerous interactions that are supposed to make the argument more coherent. When our consultant has just two ideas (which is already not bad) he expresses them in the form of a matrix. The substance of this managerial collage tends to be utterly commonplace: 'If the property market is all right, everything is all right'; 'Electricity is essential to lighting'; 'This market is mature – many consumers have already bought the product' and so on. Consultants love to invent obvious solutions, such as making savings when profits fall and diversifying when the business has cash to invest.

In the end, the adviser's role is nothing more than to make the employees accept the soundness of management's arguments for cutting back on everything and standardising terms and conditions. 'Form up in ranks!' shouts the consultant as he smashes in the unlocked door.

And then, there's a category of people that I really can't stand . . .

DUMMIES, VICTIMS AND WASTERS

Businesses like types – they find them reassuring. In business newspeak there are, first of all, the consumer families: 'adolescents', 'grannyboomers', 'ladettes' and 'dinkies' (from 'dinky' – double income, no kids yet). There are the 'leaders', the 'bobos' (from 'bourgeois bohemians') and the 'early adopters' . . . There are more every year. And since there are categories of shoppers, are there categories of workers? Why yes. There are 'experienced beginners', 'young executives', 'highly promising executives' and 'outsize executives'.

But all this kerfuffle doesn't convince me in the slightest. I would like to put forward just two classifications we can apply to the world of work. The first is mine; the second was suggested by the psychoanalyst

Jacques Lacan,[12] whose career hasn't only been spent making incomprehensible remarks for the attention of students of the unconscious. In one of his seminars, he defined the people one meets when psychoanalysts or others get together. He didn't go into great detail – that wasn't his aim – but let's hear what he suggests. You will be surprised to discover that the two classifications overlap.

The Maier classification: There are three categories: sheep, stirrers and layabouts. Sheep make up the biggest group. They take tiny steps forward, never trying to change anything, never questioning the established order, never taking any initiative that might be noticed. They are, to sum up, flaccidly inoffensive. The stirrers are the ones who screw up entire departments, creating conflict, poisoning the atmosphere and driving their colleagues to nervous breakdowns. They are rarer than the first group, fortunately, but they do much more damage. The last group – the layabouts – are the least visible. They are discreet. They harbour vague contempt for the sheep and avoid the stirrers like the plague. Their sole objective is to do as little as possible.

The Lacan classification: There are again three categories: manipulators, cynics and idiots. The manipulator likes to put himself in Other People's Shoes. In other words, he likes to direct other people's desires. The manipulator tries to control and shape those around him. It's the exploitative boss who underpays you and yet tries to make you believe he's on your side. The cynic, on the other hand, is ruled only by his own desires and doesn't try to impose them on others (in fact, what does he care for 'others'?) The cynic takes two weeks off whenever he gets the slightest cold. He fobs his work off on to other people because he has more pressing things to do – judo, women, poker, whatever. He puts his whole being into his one passion – in the great game of life, he's playing just for himself. Will he win? Well, you have to admit the cynic isn't doing badly, because he knows how to stay out of the clutches of the manipulators. These two categories – manipulators and cynics – are therefore very different from the idiots. The idiots are docile, gullible and biddable. They aren't necessarily stupid, but they let themselves get caught up in Other People's arguments. They are sufficiently malleable to let themselves be guided by whoever wants to play at being boss! In business – in fact, everywhere in life – there are legions of these perfect grunts, zealous, obsequious to those in authority, haughty to those beneath them, eager to identify with the suggested pattern of behaviour. What's more, no society could ever function without them and it is their vast number that makes any real change unlikely.

It's now time for you to find the links between these two paradigms: 'we'll look at it again in the morning'; 'don't stay up all night over it'.

THOSE YOU WILL NEVER MEET
(YOU'RE NOT MISSING ANYTHING)
Bernard Tapie and Jean-Marie Messier

There are some morons who, for two reasons, you will never come across. Firstly, because they breathe a more rarefied air than you will ever experience. Secondly, because they cross the business firmament like shooting stars before being swallowed up by black holes from which there is no escape . . .

A little history. The 1980s saw a revolution in the profile of business in French society. Until 1981 when François Mitterrand became president, business didn't get a good press in France. It was a place of exploitation and alienation. Self-made men were seen as *parvenus* in a country that placed a high value on social distinctions. Then, in a kind of vacuum of belief and grand political ambition, everything changed – well, if there's nothing else to do, let's do business!

The symbol of this enormous upheaval was Bernard Tapie, the great apostle of the cult of performance, a model of energy and darling of the media, thanks to his totally show-biz personality. I remember a baffling prime time TV show called *Ambitions* in which a powerful, determined, relaxed Bernard Tapie strode majestically along the central walkway to climb up to the podium to the rhythm of a chorus that ran: 'It's never too late to change / Be your own revolution / Whatever the weather brings / Fight for your ambitions.' To think that I was just 20 years old back then! But that's not the worst. In parallel with the consecration of the image of the champion, the mighty business manager, a highly demanding public opinion crystallised around the idea of a 'right to succeed' . . . Given the 'right to bear children' for barren women and the 'right to a sex life' for the disabled, should we soon expect a 'right to be cloned' for science freaks?

In fact, the Tapie dream didn't last very long. The business myth began to unravel around the end of the 1980s. Business failed to prevent the 1987 stock market crash or safeguard workers from rising unemployment or, still less, from the rise of Jean-Marie Le Pen's right-wing Front National. The mirage of 1980s business conditions made people believe that anyone could succeed. Today the story is much more sombre — it is possible for anyone to lose it all. That is, after all, what happened to Bernard Tapie, now a pariah in the worlds of business and politics. His career blossomed briefly, fragrant as a rose, before acquiring an unpleasant odour of dirty money and bribery. And the whole disintegration of the Tapie dream was broadcast daily on live TV in programmes such as *Opprobrium Tonight*, *Fraudsters at Ten* and *Lost Reputations News* before disappearing utterly behind the final curtain of an unsuccessful edition of *Where are they now*?

The following chapter came later in the century. It was the story of Jean-Marie Messier, a man who also got his feet caught in his giant's wings. This cuddly narcissist was first fêted then hauled over the coals. As the proverb has it, the Tarpeian Rock is just a short step from the Capitol – in other words, he was a brilliant success before he became an even more beautiful failure. Because of his swollen head, satirists started calling Messier 'J6M', standing for Jean-Marie Messier, Me Myself Momentous Master. The subject was found to be keen on having his picture taken and, in his salad days, magazines presented an admiring public with photo shoots of his 20 million euro home (paid for by Vivendi, his business) and of the leather upholstery in his private jet.

We should have guessed. It was bound to happen. He was overqualified – two French Ivy League schools. He belonged to an arrogant caste of financial controllers with experience of French government who, once they have reached a certain level, have nothing left to learn because they are the owner-managers of France and the French Incorporated.

J6M became president of an important French water supply and treatment company – CGE, rebaptised Vivendi. He could have learned all about the business – but why? Water supply is so boring. Waste water is so dirty. On the other hand, he could use the money generated by these two unsexy businesses to create a media empire out of nothing, blinding opposition with the stardust of non-existent synergies. How could he resist?

For years, the French have argued for the 'French cultural exception', in effect protecting culture – including literature, fashion, audio-visual media, journalism, academia and so on – from market forces. J6M, prophet of the new dawn, announced that the 'cultural exception' idea was dead. He was wrong. It just wasn't where we expected to find it. No, the particularity of French culture is not the aggregate impact of national identity – which makes France often unfathomable and, more rarely, wonderful – but that it so consistently finds itself swept off its feet by two-faced showmen. Remember, it was not so long ago that the bogus aristocrat but genuine Ivy Leaguer, President Valéry Giscard d'Estaing, was duped by a bloke who told him that aeroplanes in flight could smell oil in the ground . . .

V
BUSINESS IS DOOMED: WHO CAN WE BLAME?

'Globalisation risky? How do you mean?'

COULD IT BE THAT BUSINESS IS actually mortally wounded? No one believes in it any more. It keeps tripping over its own contradictions. Let's review them. (Bear in mind, this does not make me a Marxist.)

FLEXIBILITY IS THEFT

The sacrosanct rallying cry of each and every manager is flexibility. 'Cut costs,' says the company. Since the middle of the 1980s, the idea has become current that businesses are asset heavy and overstaffed — even over-furnished. This had to change. It became fashionable to contract out a large number of tasks that didn't appear to be part of the business's 'core activities'. The classic image of a modern company is a sleek centre surrounded by a vague miasma of suppliers, subcontractors, service providers, temporary staff and business partners who make it possible for employee numbers to rise and fall according to demand. The workers themselves must be organised in small, independent multidisciplinary teams answerable only to the customer.

To hear its apostles, you'd think a frenzy of change had overwhelmed business life. An interminable sequence of awareness campaigns and motivational initiatives has been rolled out so that each and every employee properly understands the 'direction' of reform and becomes a 'player' in the new administration. At the same time, departments have been repeatedly renamed, responsibilities shuffled, offices reallocated. Many people see reorganisation as a way of moving things forward, but it's also a way of justifying a salary — after all, what is the boss paid for? Well, to give the staff the impression that something — anything — is happening. In reality, everything must change so that everything can stay the same.

Conglomerates such as ABB, General Electric and IBM inspire this culture of ongoing revolution. It is to business what the Chinese Cultural Revolution was to politics: a chimerical dream of unending change. Mao Tse-Tung would be astonished to see how everything is jumbled up and called into question in an attempt to unblock the mechanism and prevent accepted practices from petrifying. That's precisely what he tried vainly to do in China, sacrificing millions of lives in the process . . . In the more comfortable — at least since 1945 — West, this idealistic, disturbing vision happily remains an imaginary utopia.

There is a downside to this abstract objective of liberating business from the base material world: redundancies. Redundancies make the business 'leaner'.

Why not get rid of that big old ugly factory? Serge Tchuruk, chief executive of the telecoms conglomerate Alcatel, nurtures just such an inspirational project: the fewer factories there are, the fewer staff there are, the fewer pay cheques there are – and the more handsomely the CEOs are rewarded. George Fisher, the head of Eastman Kodak, was responsible for the 1997 world record for showing the door (20,100 jobs lost). In the same year, he received a stock portfolio worth an estimated $60 million. Better still, Jean-Marie Messier's remuncration went up by 66 per cent in 2001 to €5.1 million while his business, Vivendi, lost €130 billion.

They rob Peter to pay Paul. The more money, personnel and factories the companies lose, the more the bosses are paid. At every step, more to some and less to others. Where will it end?

I conclude in the style of a Chinese proverb (Mao would have enjoyed this): 'The day the workers get the goat, the bosses will go under.'

TWO ARGUMENTS, ZERO INTELLIGENCE

Caught between two competing worldviews, squeezed by their contradictions, business is in trouble. On the one hand, there is the instinct to obey, on the other the urge for freedom. Let's not beat about the bush, once a company gets to a certain size, it's a stuttering behemoth, an uneasy alliance of closed fiefdoms, hunched over by tradition and habit, bound by complex salary scales and an impenetrable hierarchy of precedence. Especially in France, where the caste system is alive and well and the deciding factor in planning and carrying out any project is the network of privilege and nepotism you can call on for assistance.

And here's the paradox. The corporate behemoth also sees itself as relaxed, flexible, cool, whistling a merry tune as it sacks the workforce and reorganises to make itself more 'responsive'. It claims to wish people well but the absence of autonomy and compulsory obedience coexist with cynicism, redundancy and the reduction of the human individual to nothing more than an input. Paternalism and moral bankruptcy nourish today's tender brutality. In effect, business is a living contradiction, trying to balance the reliability of tradition with the opportunities of uncertainty, each undermining the other.

In the same way, the business worldview hesitates between systems of reference, vacillating undecided amid the twin – contradictory – positions most often put forward. The first has a whiff of Stalin's wooden tongue about it, a neo-communist argument, replete with dreams of a return to an idealised age of nationalisation, protectionism, a social contract based on infantile egalitarianism, and powerful yet doddering unions. The second stinks of the bogus cool of right-wing dynamism, the violence of its liberal discourse camouflaged by new technologies, trade, flexibility and personal development. Of course, each is a tissue of one-sided follies, but it is always fun to watch other people spouting gibberish with conviction. And then, not believing in it ourselves, we feel clever, which is always highly reassuring.

CAPITALISM: IS THERE ANYBODY THERE?

Is it possible to find people long-lasting jobs with reasonable prospects? In today's contemporary world, as my boss would say, sucking his wet lips together like a sphincter, nobody knows any more. Nevertheless, for businesses to find tolerably unstupid recruits and turn them into productive executives, they must demonstrate their usefulness to society as a whole, that the business of their business is not just lucre. For capitalism to function, like any ideological system (and it is one), it must give people reasons to act, to work, to progress. The philosopher Max Weber maintains that, at first, capitalism was steeped in the protestant work ethic. At that time, it was sustained by having 'soul', an ascetic, motivating special something, a kind of ghost of religious belief. And now? What's happened to self-fulfilment, the desire for not only just a job but a job that means something? Abandoned?

It seems so. Move along, now, there's nothing to see. There's no point in risking our lives in combat – military or economic. History is full of unnecessary battles in which people fought to the death for the right to be German or French, Catholic or Protestant. In the context of this litany of futile conflicts, aren't we better off overburdening our lives with the proliferation of insignificant pleasures offered up by our consumer society: renting a DVD at Blockbuster, buying a customised Mickey Mouse car, stuffing our faces with Ashkenazi-style beetroot delicacies from Ethnic Delights?

The writer Laurent Laurent has fun with this in the excellent *Six Months Lost in an Office:* 'You who wander the corridors with a file under your arm, I salute you! You who hang your coats close to the exit, I salute you! Yes, you who make personal phone calls . . . You, at least, will not unleash a war!' The philosopher Alexandre Kojève, a devotee of Hegel, says that, given that there are no longer any causes to get us out of bed in the morning, history is over. All that remains is for us to consume *more and more* to distinguish ourselves *more and more* from our neighbours who, in turn, look *more and more* like us.

But are these peaceful struggles and tiny satisfactions – products of a prosperous and self-satisfied liberal economy – enough to thrill our most primitive, extreme impulses? I think you have to say no. Within every one of us slumbers a choice of monster, saint, madman or hero. Tick the appropriate box and, if you feel like it, do what you have to to make it happen. But don't forget that these choices are incompatible with loading up a shopping trolley at the megamarket or chugging a beer in front of the TV after work.

ON FUTILITY AS A SECRET LAW OF HUMAN EXISTENCE

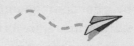

A naïve observer could easily deduce that business seeks only one thing: profit. Of course, this is sometimes true, but not always − or not only. Because, paradoxically, everyone talks about profit, but no one knows exactly what it is. It is born in the gap between what is bought and what is sold, between the merchandise and the product that finally reaches the market. Marx thought that a part of this discrepancy was value stolen by the capitalist from the worker. The reason why capitalism chases after this stolen something is perhaps because, in another way, there is pleasure hidden in the fold, in the space between what is offered and what is received, between what is taken and what is retained . . . To sum up, all humankind is made to chase after that little inaccessible extra something.

It is also a big mistake to believe that pragmatism is rational. Businesses are not governed solely by cash flow and profit-and-loss statements. It is also − more often than you'd think − a theatre of the absurd. Frequently, the action itself is the single objective of action. This is why businesses generate so much waste of time and resources. The bigger a business becomes, the more it can fritter away, right up to the point at which its ability to generate waste becomes a measure of its strength and importance. We could start by admiring the unseemly litter of utterly pointless paperwork: project descriptions, minutes from boards and meetings, mission statements, service statements, ethical contracts . . . the extravagance!

Inevitably, this profusion of documents leads to *doppelgangers*. Several people – even several teams – plough the same furrow, develop the same products, at the same time but separately. Sometimes there are even 'triplegangers' and – lets not be frightened of saying it – 'quadruplegangers'. General de Gaulle, in another context, used the pejorative French term *quarterons* to denounce a group of mutinous generals. And business is stuffed with these new-style time-serving *quarterons*. And the more there are, the more important they believe themselves to be. Which is no surprise. They are the only ones who think they actually serve a purpose.

Cost-cutting schemes never cut deep enough to excise these excesses. They are to business what love, parties and art are to life: overflowing energy and vigour looking for release. In its own special way, business appears to be following the pattern identified by the anthropologist Marcel Mauss – *potlatch*. He found that primitive peoples sought to amass enormous surpluses of wealth simply in order to waste them. 'Nothing defines humans better than their willingness to do irrational things in the pursuit of phenomenally unlikely payoffs. This is the principle behind lotteries, dating, and religion.' So says Scott Adams in *The Dilbert Principle*.

Squandering resources on the one hand, the business tries at the same time to restructure for increased efficiency. Business feels guilty! It has my sympathy. I decided to go on a severe diet after my New Year excesses, but it was too boring and I soon buried it with a few well-oiled meals, before cutting back on the *haute cuisine* once more when the weather got warmer . . . Perhaps this boom and bust cycle isn't the most effective strategy, but it certainly is the most human.

THE NEW ECONOMY: A FLASH IN THE PAN . . .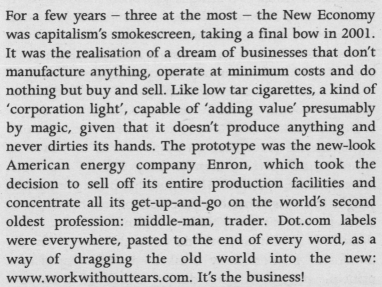

For a few years – three at the most – the New Economy was capitalism's smokescreen, taking a final bow in 2001. It was the realisation of a dream of businesses that don't manufacture anything, operate at minimum costs and do nothing but buy and sell. Like low tar cigarettes, a kind of 'corporation light', capable of 'adding value' presumably by magic, given that it doesn't produce anything and never dirties its hands. The prototype was the new-look American energy company Enron, which took the decision to sell off its entire production facilities and concentrate all its get-up-and-go on the world's second oldest profession: middle-man, trader. Dot.com labels were everywhere, pasted to the end of every word, as a way of dragging the old world into the new: www.workwithouttears.com. It's the business!

At the turn of the millennium, every dinner table had its young, ambitious, recently resigned entrepreneur on the point of creating or joining a promising business start-up. And alongside them we all felt like 'old economy' dinosaurs, stuck with our salary scales and snooze inducing career structures. Old, so very old . . . To make it worse, the new companies were so cool. There were go-kart racing weekends, video game consoles and table football in the office, youthful men and women with skateboards tucked under their arms discussing the latest rave round the water cooler.

But in 2002 Enron went bankrupt. Then WorldCom. And Jean-Marie Messier was forced to resign. Followed by Ron Sommer (Deutsche Telekom) and Robert Pittman (AOL-Time Warner). They all sold the dream before tripping over the capes of their Superman costumes with a worrying domino effect. When Enron and WorldCom fall victim to the two greatest bankruptcies in the history of the world, America stumbles. In France, things are a little different. When Vivendi or France Telecom or Alcatel are under the weather, the state coughs up as a last resort. Taxpayers pick up the tab and everything returns to normal – at a price, of course, but the end justifies the means.

Meanwhile, the mass of start-ups – created by young people convinced they had reinvented sliced bread – were washed away like sandcastles at high tide. The kids were wrong . . . So, is our economic system in danger? No, not at all, things will pick up! They always have, up to now, even if, while waiting for things to pick up, there have been some unpleasant consequences. The rise of fascism following the 1929 Crash, for example. Perhaps we need a good war. That usually works. An expensive khaki boost to the economy. Obviously, after all that destruction, there will come a time for reconstruction, will there not? Who wouldn't welcome it, I ask you?

And the moral of this story is . . . Why did the New Economy turn out to be a trap for fools? Because you can't just turn your back on the reality that tells you that a company without customers or turnover will soon be pulling down its shutters. What the hi-tech internet and telecoms crash shows us is that business chases a dream of easy money where trivial efforts bring immense rewards. The psychoanalyst would say that the business is trying to escape from its castration complex. The Marxist would say that the business is trying to elude the tendential fall in the rate of profit.

I say: 'Oh, New Economy, when will I see you again?' Like many spectators, I'm on my feet applauding when the lazy earn more money than the diligent, when the baddy wins and when the black sheep of the family marries lovely Peggy from the saloon to a soundtrack by Ennio Morricone, if you wouldn't mind . . . *But Corinne, wake up,* says the voice of reason. *Life isn't a Western. This is reality* . . . Perhaps, right there, that's the problem with economics. Insufficient dreaming.

GLOBALISATION: THERE'S A MAGGOT IN MY APPLE . . .

These days, the world is our oyster. A few decades ago in

L'Imprécateur, René-Victor Pilhes saw the future: 'It was a time when the rich nations, with their plentiful industries and countless shops, discovered a new form of faith, a project worthy of man's immemorial struggle: to turn the world into a solitary gigantic business.' Faced with the heavy artillery of the wisdom of nations, what can you say? If you don't get it, what use are you? You are obsolete. Individuals are the world, businesses are the world, states are the world. The world is the sole storehouse of raw materials, the workers' only habitat, a global common market, like a huge financial game board. Worldwide union beneath the banner of a single dream: of oneness, of sameness. Everywhere the same brands, the same products, the same people. The 21st century will be international or there won't be one. That's the liberals' rallying cry and there's nothing revolutionary about it. Could it just be a new way to visualise the final struggle?

And all that is necessary. It must be. Will the end of history take free market form, its tentacles multiplying, stretching further and further, across the sea, across frontiers? I've already said how the German philosopher Hegel believed that human social evolution was not infinite, but would come to a halt when humanity achieved a form of society that satisfied its deepest, most primary needs. The problem is, all that the 20th century put forward as necessary turned out to be – fundamentally – totalitarian. We should be extremely wary. Consider the laws of history that communism is supposed to have obeyed. Consider the laws of nature that

Nazism is alleged to have followed. Should we now believe in the law of profit that governs capitalism?

Fortunately, voices are being raised in opposition. From the ranks of the apostles of globalisation, there are more and more desertions. Some of the capitalist system's most dynamic henchmen have noisily swapped sides in the last few years, a few big fish among them. None bigger than the speculator George Soros – who, let's not forget, owes his colossal fortune to the independence of the financial markets – and the Nobel Prize-winning economist Joseph Stiglitz,[13] former vice president of the World Bank. (A short digression: God knows why but public opinion and the media are always first and foremost interested in whistle-blowers. Given that *Bonjour Laziness* blows the whistle on business, will it bring me success? I wonder . . .) Anti-globalisation is fashionable, it seems! And if it worries people who have been its most ardent supporters or its most crucial protagonists, there can be no doubt that there's a maggot in the apple. And if nothing is done to stop it, that little maggot will grow bigger and bigger . . .

THERE IS NO DOWNSIDE TO DISENGAGEMENT

'How many work in my department?''
On a good day probably about half.'

IF THERE IS NO UPSIDE TO WORKING, you don't have much to lose by twiddling your thumbs. Doing nothing will undermine your employer – and without risk to yourself. It would be a shame not to seize this opportunity. No more career, no more authority, no more work either. *Carpe diem*! But making people still think you are busy isn't necessarily easy . . .

WORK AND THE END OF THE CAREER

There are no more careers. Many executives no longer really know what they are paid for. Whole areas of activity and numerous posts (advisers, experts, managers) serve no purpose, none at all. Except, maybe, 'managing' paperwork, showing off with powerpoint presentations and trying to dazzle in meetings. There are legions of utterly redundant tasks: drafting policy guidelines for writing software code; taking part in a working party on the development of a suggestions system for improving products; attending a seminar entitled 'Imagineering integrated solutions at international level and on a global scale'. Not forgetting designing new forms and new procedures. Or writing reports of more than two pages (which no one will ever read). Or, better still, 'line managing' projects – the majority of which will fail or will end up having nothing to do with the idea you started with.

What's more, the holders of these meaningless posts cleverly cloud the issue. What does the general public make of a 'knowledge manager' or a 'quality supervisor' or a 'standardisation implementation manager'? Next time you go out to dinner, just try this. Tell people 'I work for a big company.' You'll see. No one will ask you what you do, not even who you work for. Not even out of pity.

Even secretaries no longer have a trade – when there are any left, that is, because they are in danger of extinction. It takes a Michel Houellebecq – an author capable of lyricism even when writing about the office landscape of our fine, competitive French businesses – to write:

'Executives climb to Calvary
In lifts of solid nickel.
I see the passing secretary
Freshening her lashes with Rimmel.'

But the denizen of the 1960s' typing pool, in glasses and miniskirt, obedience personified behind her monolithic typewriter, is no more than a distant memory. By 'squeezing' staff numbers, we have lost, some say, numerous opportunities for adultery, replacing them with well-tempered bureaucratic puritanism focused solely on the pleasures of the screen. Those who survived the great office IT revolution now have diplomas and do the same jobs you do: they sort, file and produce paperwork.

The secretary is not there to serve you. That isn't so much a mistake as an unpardonable error – for which you will not be forgiven. Because secretaries suffer from a huge inferiority complex – arising out of the undeserved contempt of French society for so-called 'menial' tasks – you have to make yourself particularly agreeable to them. There is little kudos in directly serving another person and those who carry out this kind of task feel a sense of failure. In turn, they seldom show initiative or efficiency, determined as they are to be nobody's 'lackey'. The trouble is, we are all, more or less, someone else's lackey. To serve without servility – that is the question, the test . . . What is the *mot juste*? Ah yes, the challenge!

The typist has disappeared but the work she used to do hasn't. In part, you do it yourself. The holiday calendar, invoice control, customer relations, hotel and transport bookings, small maintenance jobs, the post. *Bonjour* chores! And there are so many of them that ever so subtly they transformed themselves from means to an end into an end in themselves. If you make a post redundant, the work just has to be done by somebody else – QED – by managers working 'two for the price of one'. If it isn't 'three for the price of one', because the reduction in the number of degrees in the company hierarchy means fewer and fewer bosses and your job as middle manager now requires you also to become your own secretary and boss. Holy business Trinity, hear the prayers of executives overburdened with paperwork . . .

In reality, though, you have never been as free as you are in this demented paper chase, precisely because of the clouds of uncertainty surrounding the tasks handed down to you. Nobody knows exactly what you do. If anyone ever asks, whatever you do, don't tell them you spend your days organising your paperwork into neat piles.

NO MORE AUTHORITY: WHEN THE CAT'S AWAY . . .

'No one knows what's going on. Everything's a mess. There's nobody in charge, no respect for anything. It'll all end in tears. What we need is strong leadership . . .' That's what they all say, those who pine for the 'good old days'. It's not just in family life that authority is lacking — it simply isn't fashionable any more. This dehiscence (yes, I do like rare words that my superiors don't understand) worries psychoanalysts, concerns educationalists and makes teachers tear their hair out.

Me, I rub my hands with glee. What a lucky break! As a manager, no one will ever give you a direct order. No one will ever tell you that you are an incompetent idiot. In business, a permissive, friendly atmosphere is compulsory. It is, however, no less oppressive for all that — but the form taken by oppression is consensus, blessed consensus. The important thing is to respect the rules and rites – the *status quo* – more important than either the business itself or its objectives. The means and the ends have been reversed.

What does that mean in everyday life? Your boss will give out some lame opinion. Everyone nods vaguely or picks up on some secondary aspect. A few people turn their minds to what they will have for dinner that evening. Everyone ends up agreeing. What is paramount is the compulsion to do nothing that might undermine the cohesion of the group. The super smooth business world is no place for calling a spade a spade. Acquiescence is, don't forget, a condition of access to the higher echelons. Unanimity is crystallised in meetings – meetings, bleating meetings and schmeetings. But really, communing with the spirit of the group, sacrificing common sense (which I'm afraid isn't all that common), is that really work? Come along now. Be serious. Yes, it's a chore. Accommodating other people's views is, by definition, difficult. But it isn't work.

The prime objective of any business is to make the employee voluntarily take on things which ought to be imposed from outside. This new-style pressure tactic takes the form imagined by the English visionary Jeremy Bentham, the eighteenth century inventor of the panopticon prison. In a panopticon, a single person, in a kind of central hide, can oversee hundreds, even thousands of people. Nobody knows when they are being watched – if at all – because the invisible *gauleiter* has perhaps nipped off to the loo. According to the philosopher Michel Foucault, the panopticon might even be the modern archetype for all forms of power, in business and elsewhere: impenetrable and all embracing.

Because there is no real authority – because an omnipresent, impersonal system has drowned it – there is no longer any form of debate. There's a phrase you often hear from people who don't agree with the one-party state line imposed by their boss: 'You can't just tell him like that.' But because you can't just tell him like that, nobody tells him anything at all – or they do so in such a mealy-mouthed way that what they are saying loses its bite, their arguments lose their impact. Form up in ranks. Face front, shoulders back. Mouths shut.

AND NO MORE WORK: OH, JOY . . .

So who does work in business? Let's peer behind the curtain. Apparently, no one much. On this very subject, I have an extremely instructive story to relate. A small number of French companies are in the habit of competing with one another in a rowing race with four oarsmen and one coxswain. The teams are made up of employees of each company. One set of managers notices that their team always comes last. Cue rending of garments and an inquest. The company employs a sports consultant to find out what is going on. At the end of several weeks' work, the expert concludes that, in this boat, there are four coxes and only one oarsman. The management is confounded. They ask a consultant for advice. The nub of the advice is that the oarsman is insufficiently motivated! Any similarity to actual companies, living or dead, is, of course, purely coincidental . . . In fact, firms often tend to resemble the Mexican army, an inefficient organisation in which everyone wants to be the boss, the 'line manager' or the 'team leader', but no one wants to carry out the orders.

What this short parable shows is that, in France, no one lifts a damn finger. This is one of the less well-known facets of the 'French cultural exception'. The total amount of work done in mainland France is incredibly low relative to the population. You don't need statistics to prove it. Simply take a stroll on any weekday along St Germain des Prés. There are people everywhere, many of them sauntering adults of working age capable of contributing to the country's economic might. The country, however, has no need of them. French productivity is one of the highest in the world. As a consequence, working life lasts just 30 short years, unemployment remains high and the sacrosanct long weekends around the May bank holidays turn into nearly a week if the day off falls on a Wednesday. As for the governmental programme for a shorter working week, that chips away still further in favour of greater and greater demands for free time.

So why do managers constantly gripe about not having enough time? Because they pretend to work ever-longer hours, always nose to the grindstone. It is, I admit, sometimes true. For sub-contractors for example, as we've already seen, who work to extremely strict standards with their continuing business at stake. It's also true for the mindless idiots who have accepted taking on operational responsibilities 'on the ground' or 'at the customer interface', constantly juggling deadlines, caught between the conflicting demands of the market and their company – seriously, you'd have to be a masochist to put up with conditions like these. It isn't surprising that those who accept them risk *karochi* – the uniquely Japanese sudden death of an executive in the prime of life – or the less serious *burn out*, a kind of stress-related exhaustion peculiar to the workforces of the English-speaking economies.

It's a fact. Work is distributed so unfairly that a handful of individuals sweat blood so that the majority can live the life of Reilly. Executives with qualifications from good or average graduate schools, who have managed to hide themselves away in some sheltered spot in a big organisation, will tell you they are snowed under with work. They are lying. Other – craftier – customers dress it up skilfully such as Jean-Cyril Spinetta, the chief executive of Air France. In an interview in March 2003, he revealed, with a frankness that does him credit: 'I organise my time to ensure periods of disconnection.' Translation? 'Some of the time I do bugger all.' Well done. Tell it like it is. Work is dead – long live work!

DOING NOTHING IS AN ART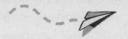

Your boss brings nothing to the table but his or her time – they are, simply, present. But then they add a layer of pretence – they are overwhelmed with work! Their body language suggests that they pay a physical price for their devotion to the cause. Unlike in Germany, where employees who leave work late are considered inefficient, in France and many other countries you look good if you only 'slip away' once eight or even nine o'clock has sounded. Thus proving you love your work. Of course that means that, in some big companies, members of staff stay late, interminably cloistered in their offices, making personal phone calls, surfing the internet, using the photocopier and reading the paper. At least they aren't working.

But doing nothing isn't easy: you have to know how to pretend. Here's the appropriate advice from the infallible Scott Adams's precious guide *The Dilbert Principle*: 'Never go out into the corridors without a file tucked under your arm. Employees with their arms full of paperwork look like they are on their way to important meetings. Those who carry nothing look like they are on the way to the canteen. Those carrying a newspaper appear to be on the way to the toilets. Above all, never forget to take lots of files home from work with you each evening. You will thus give the false impression that you are doing lots of overtime.' Now you know what to do to do nothing.

You can also spend your days collecting information in meetings and passing it on down the line. Take care not to append any kind of added-value because that would be working. A recent study from the USA discovered that, on average, the executives surveyed received 85 emails per day. The vast majority, you can be sure, served no purpose whatsoever. But this avalanche of messages presents three advantages: they provide employment for 'network managers'; they keep the people who send them busy; they keep the people who receive them busy.

For the most ambitious among you, you must always be on the lookout for when a big cheese goes by in the corridor. This is the obsession of the listless Adrien Deume, a character in Albert Cohen's mythical novel *Belle du seigneur*. Deume is a mid-ranking civil servant with a single dream: with his well-shined shoes and by dint of sheer hard work, he hopes to haul himself up the hierarchy to level A where he will be eligible for a rewarding post at the League of Nations (the forerunner of the UN censured by de Gaulle). Meanwhile his wife, the lovely Ariane, enthusiastically cuckolds him with his boss, the jovial Solal: it is thus proved that there is justice inherent in novels as well as in organisations.

CONCLUSION

START TOMORROW –
BRING YOUR
COMPANY DOWN

© CartoonStock

'He's our ideas man – I can never tell
if he's working or not.'

THE TRIAL IS ENDED, judgement has been handed down, the hearing is over. You never will be a corporate 'new man'. Business will have to do without another honest, faithful servant, selflessly devoted to the common goal, a pawn to those in power, a willing slave, a worthy inheritor, yoked to the needs of the team. Your company aims to enslave you body and soul, but achieves the opposite effect. It reveals a pattern of oppression to which your only sane response is implacable apathy, discreetly but unwaveringly leeching its resources.

Rather than a 'new man', be a blob, a leftover, stubbornly resisting the pressure to conform, impervious to manipulation. Become the grain of sand that seizes up the whole machine, the sore thumb. Free yourself from the relentless demands of usefulness, the incontestable, impersonal common good — none of this ever made a single individual really happy.

White-collar dissidents, the time has come to disengage!

TEN CORPORATE COMMANDMENTS
FOR MIDDLE MANAGEMENT

Let's sum up. This is what the company expects of its middle managers — substantial, sometimes contradictory, expectations. To meet them, it's best not to give them too much thought. Good luck with that.

And don't be surprised if the company talks down to you. You're just a tool, an instrument for the organisation to exploit.

1. Work is an asset, employment a privilege. If you have a job, you're lucky — many people don't.
2. Give your time freely or you won't find — or keep — a steady job.
3. The company expects the earth and owes you nothing in return. That's just how it is — the 'hard economic reality'. You have no choice because there is no future, no society, no life or form of accomplishment that does not derive from work and employment.
4. Respect the rules of the game. Everyone is equal in business. Only the best, therefore, will triumph. The current rules were implemented by the highest-ranking — and, thus, the most competent — people. If, in your turn, you fail to succeed, it isn't because the dice are loaded, it's because you don't deserve success. When you fail, you will have only yourself to blame.

5. Remain biddable, flexible. Consensus is paramount. It's better to be wrong in company than right all alone. What counts is everybody staying in step, regardless of the direction taken or the methods employed. The finger of blame will point out anyone who flouts the party line.

6. Don't believe too much in what you do. There's no point. It might even be counterproductive. People who take their work too seriously stop the rest of us peacefully drifting in circles. They are fanatics, a danger to the system.

7. Accept the corporate world just as it is. The majority of executives you run into are white, middle class, heterosexuals from authentic French stock – the more senior ones are men. Don't be surprised. Foreigners have fewer paper qualifications than the French, gays have more problems with integration than other people, women devote less time to their work than men do etc. Repeat after me.

8. Recite out loud like you mean it – global conglomeration is *necessary;* businesses need *flexibility;* unemployment for unskilled workers is *here to stay;* our pension system costs society *far too much*. When you get to the end, start over until you are certain of every syllable.

9. Buy into the executive's creed: tomorrow belongs to responsive companies networking with multiple partners, whose internal organisation is team or project based and focused on customer satisfaction. To 'stay afloat' in an 'uncertain', 'complex' business ocean, there is no alternative. If you don't believe all

this, there's no point in you coming to work tomorrow.

10. Use the following words sparingly: structure, function, career, management, plans, objectives, hierarchy, status. These words are no longer fashionable. Of course, if you work in a major company, they continue to exist, muddled in with the previous commandment, which doesn't help. But it's up to you to make the best of it, son. What do you think they pay you for?

To shatter the ten stone tablets of corporate commandments, I would like to propose a different paradigm. I will not speak down to you. You aren't just a reader. You are a person.

1. These days slaves are not branded, they are given a salary. Never forget that there is no scope for personal fulfilment at work — if there was, we would have noticed. You work for your pay cheque at the end of the month — full stop (as we say in business).

2. There is no point in trying to change the system. Opposing it will make it stronger. Arguing against it stiffens its resolve. You can, of course, enjoy yourself with anarchic practical jokes. You could institute a special day for calling in sick or steal the office stationery because the office has stolen your life. Yes, it's fun, but revolution was all very well for the militants of the 1970s — look where they are now! (On the board.)

3. Nothing you do makes any difference. You can be replaced at a moment's notice by the first available idiot. So, work as little as possible but put a modicum of effort – not too much, though – into 'selling yourself' and 'networking'. If you get it right, when the inevitable reorganisation comes along, you will be untouchable (and untouched).

4. You will not be judged on how well you do your job, but on your carefully rehearsed ability to appear to be doing your job. The more meaningless jargon you use, the more people will respect you.

5. Never, for any reason, should you accept a position of responsibility. If you do, you'll be obliged to do masses more work for just a few measly notes more – if that!

6. In the biggest companies, choose the least useful jobs – consultancy, mentoring, research, report writing. The more pointless the job, the more difficult it is for anyone to quantify your 'contribution to the wealth of the company'. Avoid operational, hands-on positions like the plague. The ideal solution is to get yourself promoted sideways into some unproductive – often cross-departmental – post, where the work has no impact on anything and there is no pressure from above to perform: cushti.

7. Should you be lucky enough to find such a cushy billet, avoid change that could get you noticed. They can only fire the executives they can find.

8. Learn to recognise the discreet signals – unusual clothes, bad jokes, warm smiles – that identify those who share your doubts about the system, who have

noticed just how absurd it is.

9. Make sure you are polite to any temporary staff you are given 'responsibility' for – short-term contractors, temps, outside service providers. Remember, they are the only people who ever do any real work.

10. Keep telling yourself that the whole ridiculous corporate ideology is no more 'real' than the communist system's dialectical materialism. When its time comes, it will – inevitably – crumble. As Stalin said, in the end, death wins. If only we knew when . . .

NOTES

[1] I am a little unkind here. The truth is, I'm jealous. Although my cushy corner of business is better paid than theirs, it has less class. I admit that some academics – mostly sociologists – have written work on companies worthy of attention.

[2] What, exactly? OK, confession time: psychoanalysis and writing. But there are loads of other captivating occupations (paid or not, that isn't the point): breeding donkeys, building the perfect hi-fi system, organising parties, volunteering, growing grapes, trading fossils, painting, cruising on the beach . . .

[3] From an IFOP survey for Gallup, quoted in the magazine *Enjeux-Les Echos*, issue 187, dated January 2003.

[4] *Extension du domaine de la lutte*, Editions J'ai lu, August 2005, published as *Whatever*, trans. Paul Hammond (Serpent's Tail, London 1998)

[5] '*Avant-garde* financial daily' – a fine example of an oxymoron, as will be seen, my favourite figure of speech (cf *Business culture*).

[6] Published in the UK as £9.99, trans. Adriana Hunter (Picador, London, 2002).

[7] The author of *Liberation Management* – another oxymoron! It goes without saying that you shouldn't read it.

[8] Yes, it's true, I like pop music. Here I will adopt as hymn the work of Georges Archier, Olivier Elissalt and Alain Setton in *Mobiliser pour Réussir* – published by Editions du Seuil in 1989: –'Circles

of quality will highly motivate you / Our methods will draw respect from you / Volunteering will be fostered by you / Impatience will be mastered by you / Teamwork will be promoted by you / But there'll be no interference by you / Absolute confidence will be shown by you / Greed will be banished by you / A vocation will be sought by you.'

9 *Dogbert, méthodes ultrasecrètes pour diriger une enterprise.* Published in English as *Dogbert's Top Secret Management Handbook* (Boxtree, London, 1997).

10 Translator's note: *L'Imprécateur* was published in English in 1978 by Marion Boyars Publishers under the title *The Provocateur.*

11 You can see the impact of May 1968 here! Business absorbs everything, even ideas which, confronting an ossified hierarchy of power, at one time seemed an emancipation.

12 I refer the reader to one of my books, *Le Divan c'est amusant* (Psychoanalysis is Fun), published by Michalon in 2005.

13 *George Soros on Globalisation*, Public Affairs, 2004; and Joseph Stiglitz, *Globalization and Its Discontents,* Norton, 2003.

FURTHER READING

NOVELS

Frédéric Beigbeder, £9.99, trans. Adriana Hunter (Picador, London: 2002)

Thierry Beinstingel, *Central* (Fayard, Paris: 2000)

Albert Cohen, *Belle du seigneur*, trans. David Coward (Penguin, London: 1997)

Don DeLillo, *Americana* (Penguin, London: 1990)

Béatrice Hammer, *L'édifiante histoire de Green.com* (A. Contrario: 2004)

Michel Houellebecq, *Whatever*, trans. Paul Hammond (Serpent's Tail, London: 1998)

—*Poésies* (Le Seuil, Paris: 1999)

Laurent Laurent, *Six mois au fond d'un bureau* (Le Seuil, Paris: 2001)

René-Victor Pilhes, *The Provocateur*, trans. Denver and Helen Lindley (Marion Boyars, London: 1978)

François Salvaing, *La Boîte* (Fayard, Paris: 1998)

Françoise Verny, *Le plus beau métier du monde* (Orban, Paris: 1990)

NON-FICTION

Scott Adams, *The Dilbert Principle: A Cubicle's-Eye View of Bosses, Meetings, Management Fads and Other Workplace Afflictions* (Boxtree, London: 1996)

—*Dogbert's Top Secret Management Handbook* (Boxtree, London: 1997)

Christian Boltanski and Eve Chiapello, *Le Nouvel Esprit du capitalisme* (Gallimard, Paris: 1999)

Marie-Anne Dujarier, *Il faut réduire les affectifs: Petit lexique de management* (Mots et Cie: 2001)

Alain Ehrenberg, *L'Individu incertain* (Calmann-Lévy: 1995)

Barbara Ehrenreich, *Nickel and Dimed: Undercover in Low-wage USA* (Granta, London: 2002)

André Gorz, *Reclaiming Work: Beyond the Wage-Based Society*, trans. Chris Turner (Polity, Cambridge: 1999)

Philippe d'Iribarne, *La logique de l'honneur: gestion des enterprises et traditions nationals* (Le Seuil, Paris: 1989)

Naomi Klein, *No Logo: No Space, No Choice, No Jobs* (Flamingo, London: 1999)

Jean-Pierre Le Goff, *Le mythe de l'entreprise* (La Découverte: 1992)

—*La Barbarie douce* (La Découverte: 1999)

Yves Pagès, *Petites natures mortes au travail* (Verticales: 2000)

Nicolas Riou, *Comment j'ai foiré ma start-up* (Éditions d'Organisation: 2001)

Richard Sennett, *The Corrosion of Character: the Personal Consequences of Work in the New Capitalism* (Norton,

New York: 1998)

George Soros, *George Soros on Globalization* (Public Affairs: 2002)

Joseph Stiglitz, *Globalization and Its Discontents* (Norton, New York: 2003)

Françoise Thom, *Newspeak: The Language of Soviet Communism*, trans. Ken Connelly (Claridge, London: 1989)

Raoul Vaneigem, *Adresse aux vivants: sur la mort qui les gouverne et l'opportunité de s'en défaire* (Seghers: 1990)

MISCELLANEOUS

Pierre Dac, *Essais, maximes et conférences* (Le Cherche Midi: 1978)

Enjeux-Les Échos, le Mensuel de l'Économie

Without forgetting: Pierre Carles's film *Attention, danger travail*

MORE GENERALLY

I have also made reference to: Hannah Arendt, *The Human Condition*; Guy Debord, *Society of the Spectacle*; Michel Foucault, *Discipline and Punish*; Sigmund Freud, *Civilisation and its Discontents*; René Girard, *Violence and the Sacred*; Alexandre Kojève, *Introduction to the Reading of Hegel*; Jacques Lacan, *The Ethics of Psychoanalysis*; Christopher Lasch, *The Culture of Narcissism*; Marcel Mauss, *The Gift*; Karl Marx, *Capital*; George Orwell, *1984*; Donatien-Alphonse-François de Sade, *Philosophy in the Boudoir*; Max Weber, *The Protestant Ethic and the Spirit of Capitalism*.